MW00975058

The *Son* seventh

ROY BRADIE BRANNON

The  seventh
Son

TATE PUBLISHING
AND ENTERPRISES, LLC

This book is designed to provide accurate and authoritative information with regard to the subject matter covered. This information is given with the understanding that neither the author nor Tate Publishing, LLC is engaged in rendering legal, professional advice. Since the details of your situation are fact dependent, you should additionally seek the services of a competent professional.

The opinions expressed by the author are not necessarily those of Tate Publishing, LLC.

Published by Tate Publishing & Enterprises, LLC
127 E. Trade Center Terrace | Mustang, Oklahoma 73064 USA
1.888.361.9473 | www.tatepublishing.com

Tate Publishing is committed to excellence in the publishing industry. The company reflects the philosophy established by the founders, based on Psalm 68:11,
"The Lord gave the word and great was the company of those who published it."

Book design copyright © 2015 by Tate Publishing, LLC. All rights reserved.
Cover design by Ivan Charlem Igot
Interior design by Mary Jean Archival

Published in the United States of America

ISBN: 978-1-68118-560-6
Biography & Autobiography / General
15.03.13

How Good Food Turned My Health Around

Born on a rural farm in Southern Floyd County, Georgia, April 4, 1940, the seventh son of eight boys and three girls. Out of a family of eleven kids, you had to learn early to take care of yourself. Life was hard and we had no electricity for several years of my early life. We were very poor and had very little but we had plenty of good food and very seldom sick and we were happy. Talk about a lot of humorous stories about my family and I. Tell about a severe injury to my leg and my health deteriorated so bad I almost gave up and threw in the towel and die. Read the book Wheat Belly and how it turned my health completely around. Today *I am medicine free.* Years of taking medicine for diabetics, high blood pressure, and high cholesterol, and now no medicine. Don't give up and throw in the towel. Last of the old timers who saw time go from a hard simple life to very modern world that we live in today.

The Seventh Son

Born on a small farm in a rural community of Rome, Georgia, in Floyd County, April 4, 1940, I was the seventh son of a family of eleven children. I understand the seventh sons are the lucky ones. This story is about the struggles and hardship of growing up in the South during this era. I am also comparing the food and other related topics of that time to what we have now.

We lived in a wood frame house on Pullen Road. This got a little crowded as the family grew. While I was growing up, I hardly ever saw anyone that was overweight. I would say that probably around 75 percent of people were average weight at least. That was yesterday but today I believe about 75 percent of people today are overweight. I was the last to be born at home. My mother and my sister, Sarah La

Rue, were in the hospital at the same time. Ten months later, my sister, Barbara and my niece, Elizabeth LaRue, were born. Dad also owned a house on US27 about two miles from the farm and he moved us over there.

When I was around four years old, Grady was also born in a hospital. Aunt Mary Ellen Brannon lived close by and she said everyone was very excited to see Grady come home in an ambulance. I can still see that ambulance pulling up to our house. Polio was the number one fear in those days and now cancer is number one fear today why? We lived in a wood frame house and we heated the entire house with a fireplace and we all gathered around the fireplace to try and stay warm. Also we used kerosene lamps for light. When we went to bed dad would put a backlog (a large stick of wood) in the fireplace, and if we were lucky, there would still be some fire in the fireplace in the morning. Dad would throw more wood on the fire and soon we would have a good fire going to help keep us warm. If the fire went out in the fireplace, Dad would get small strips of heart pine and place them in the fireplace and then lay small sticks of wood on them. He would light the heart pine, which was easy to get started. After the fire got going good, he then would place larger wood in the fireplace.

One thing you learned early in life was how to start a fire in the fireplace. Early in the morning, the temperature outside was maybe 5 degrees warmer inside. At night Mom would take the iron that she had ironed our clothes with and set it on the wood stove or next to the fire in the fireplace to get it hot then wrap it in towels and put it in bed with us. I was lucky I slept inside with my grandmother, Anna Cargle. My brothers Glenn and Earl slept on the open back porch. Yes, the temperature was the same. My grandmother Anna was a full-blooded Cherokee Indian and she was a short slim lady with long black hair. My brothers Earl and Glenn would take a crosscut saw and cut firewood regardless of the weather. For some reason, Dad never did store wood for the winter and he waited until the last minute to cut our firewood. He would cut down trees and take the mules and pull them to the backyard.

Earl was promoted to milking the cows and my younger brother Grady helped me cut firewood. Years later we started using a warm morning heater and we used coal to heat with. This was a lot better heating system. They loaded the heater with coal for the night and they forgot to close the damper. You controlled the heat by adjusting the air flow with the damper and the more air the faster the heater would get hot. It took longer to get coal started and you would give it more air. The heater was in the living room and for some reason no one was close by. All of a sudden the heater sounded like a tornado even though it was clear outside. Everyone ran into the living room to see what was happening. They had forgotten to close the damper and the heater was getting too much air. The stove pipe was bright red and making lots of noise. I was scared I thought the house was going to catch on fire and burn down. Dad ran over, closed the damper, and the heater started cooling down real fast. Thank goodness we had a double wall pipe running through the wood wall and if it had lasted a few more minutes it would have set the house on fire. Can you imagine pulling buckets of water up out of a well over a hundred feet away to put the fire out? I don't think so. We had no fire department in the county and we had no insurance. It was our lucky day.

Grace used a wood stove for cooking and just above the stove was a place to sit leftovers and they would stay warm. On the side of the stove was a water tank and that is where we got our hot water.

The iceman ran once a week. They would use ice hooks and bring two chunks of ice and put them in the icebox. The ice would not last all week, and when we ran out, we would take our Coke and milk down to the well. Then we would put them down into the well. This would at least keep the drinks cool.

On one hot summer day, Grady and I went down to get some cokes. We were running back to the house when one of the Cokes blew up and cut Grady's upper lip completely in two. They had to take Grady to McCall Hospital in Rome. It took several stitches to sew up Grady's lip. Life was hard but we were very seldom sick.

The War Is Over

When I was six years old, my three oldest brothers came home from World War II. John, the oldest, fought with Gen. George Patton's Army. John would not talk much about the war but John did tell a few of his war stories.

He said, "I was point man and they came up on some Germans and the Germans opened fire on them I took cover behind a dirt embankment. I felt safe and all of a sudden bullets were hitting all around me."

The Americans were shooting at the Germans and almost shot him and they shot his gun in two. After this battle was over, John was left behind German lines. John went to a farm house and had the French farmers hide him. John had plenty of army rations and he shared it with the farmer, his wife, and children as they had no food.

John said, "I was scared because I could hear Germans talking and walking around outside the house. If they had found me in the house they would of have kill the Frenchmen for sure and probably me also."

After about a week the Germans left. John found his unit, walked to where they were, and cussed them out and told them they almost killed him and left him behind enemy lines. They had charged him with desertion and the captain said, "We were going to court-martial you for desertion if you had not come in a and cussed us out."

John said, "We were in small town fighting the Germans and they had brought up a tank and it was coming down this small street into town." He said, "They had nothing to stop that tank with and I was so scared that I knew I was going to die. And out of fear for my life I ran jumped up on the tank jerked the tank hatch open and pointed my gun at the drive and I said stop and he did. I ordered them out of the tank and I had captured a tank and three Germans."

They were going to honor him with the Medal of Honor for bravery. John told them, "Hell no, you are not, I did not do it out of bravery, I did it because I was scared as hell." John said, "We were marching at night and it was so dark you could not see anything. I had my hand on the soldier in front of me. We all marched that way. All of a sudden, it lit up like daylight. We had marched into a U-shaped big gun emplacement. The Germans opened fire on us. It sounded like bees flying around me. The bullets shot my riffle into and

I hit the dirt. I dug a foxhole the fastest I had ever dug one. One of our solders was wounded real bad and he laid out their hollering 'Moma, Moma.' A medic tried to go treat him and he got killed. After that there was nothing we could do for him. After hours of listening to that poor solider hollering, I decided to get out there. The Germans brought mules in and started pulling the big guns back. I motioned to a buddy of mine. My buddy and I were crawling along and came up on a German in a foxhole. We caught him by surprise and my buddy pointed his rifle at him and motioned arms up. I told him get us out of here, the German understood English. The next morning I went with more soldiers to rescue our boys. The young soldier that laid there hollering 'Moma' had died."

After the war was over, John came home to visit and we were very excited. I was outside shooting firecrackers. John gave me fifty cents not to shoot firecrackers. In those days, fifty cents was a lot of money. Later in life, I understood why he paid me not to shoot firecrackers.

John had served several years in the Army and he would send his pay home so he could buy a house when he got out of the Army. John was married to Mildred Roper and had one son, Larry, before he went into the Army. When John came home after the war, Mildred had been running around on him and spent all his money. John divorced her and married Jewell Slay and they had two beautiful girls, Bonnie and Sherry.

George "Doc," the second oldest son, fought the Japanese in the Pacific theater. He was in the Navy. While Doc was in training he did something wrong and was ordered to stand at attention and hold his riffle straight out. He was told if he let his arms down he was in serious trouble. After what seemed like hours of standing out in the hot sun, he said, "The rifle felt like it weighed a hundred pounds. I thought I couldn't take it much longer." A few minutes later a lieutenant came walking by and whispered, "Pass out and fall down." Doc did, and they came running and took care of him. Doc was stationed on a minesweeper and it was anchored off a small island when the Japanese opened fire on them. Doc said, "I was standing on the back of the ship when all of a sudden a shell exploded about a hundred yards in front of us. The lieutenant said, 'Doc, pick up that ax and cut the anchor cable.' Soon another shell exploded a lot closer. I picked up the ax and the first time I cut the cable in two. I knew they were zeroing in on us. The lieutenant said, 'Let's get the hell out of here.' The captain told the lieutenant, 'You cannot cut the anchor cable and you could be court-martialed for that.' The lieutenant told the captain, 'I have a wife and two kids back home and I will go home to see them.'"

Another time Doc was on the back of the minesweeper and they were pulling the anchor up. Doc said, "Just in time I saw a mine being pulled toward the ship and I started hollering stop, stop and they stopped just in time or we all would have been killed." Doc said, "We were out patrolling for mines when we found a wounded Japanese solder. We brought him aboard and treated his wounds. We took good care of him." The captain called the Marines and told them what was going on. They said when we got close to shore they will send a small boat out to get the prisoner. This small boat came up and a Marine sergeant came aboard. Doc carried him to where the prisoner was and he reached down, picked up the prisoner, and threw him over his shoulder. He went over to his boat and dropped him in the boat. "I asked, 'Hey, what are you doing?' He said, 'You can't kill them.' I did not like it but there was nothing I could do. I have always wondered what happened to that prisoner."

James "Shag," the third oldest, fought the Americans and "Shag" was not mean, he was just very mischievous. Shag could keep you laughing and everyone liked him. He was just always doing crazy things. Shag first went into the Air Force and while he was in training during target practice he was shooting at buzzards, a no-no. The captain asked Shag why he was shooting at the buzzards. Shag said, "Sir, I thought they were enemy planes." The captain said, "I got a job for you." He carried Shag over to where a bunch of small oak trees were. Now remember Shag was stationed in the desert in Arizona. The captain points to an area where he wants the oaks set out. Shag said, "The only other thing growing was cactus."

The captain gave Shag strict orders: "Don't let them oaks die and you had better keep lots of water on them."

Shag said, "There was one big problem it was very hot and dry and when I poured water around the trees and the water would just disappeared in the hot sand as fast as I poured it."

Soon Shag was transferred to the Army. The Air Force had kicked him out. Another time Shag and one of his buddies tried to sneak out of camp and go into town for the night. Shag told me, "They were crawling on their belly so they would not be spotted sneaking out of camp. All of a sudden, I felt some boots and looked up and it was my old sergeant." He said, "Hello, Sarge," another no-no. Shag spent over a hundred days in the brig. Shag had bedded down for the night and someone hollered, "Brannon, it's your turn to turn out the lights." Shag picked up his boot, threw it, and knocked the lights out. Well, back to the brig. If "Shag" was not in the brig, he was doing KP peeling potatoes. Shag had hurt his leg during training and while he was marching to the ship to go overseas his leg swelled up on him. Shag could not walk so he missed the boat. The war was already in its closing days.

Farm Life

After the war was over, there was a severe shortage of automobiles. With all the men returning home from the war, they wanted automobiles. Factories had been producing things to fight the war with and it took time to switch over to civilian use. Doc ordered a car and it was going to take over a year to get one. Dad would hook the mules up to the wagon and we would take a load of corn to Cedartown, Georgia, to have it ground into corn meal. It was an all-day trip. I will never forget my first train ride. Dad wanted us to ride the train to Cedartown. We needed some salt and coffee and a few other things so Dad, Glenn, Earl, and I walked about three miles east and over to the relay train station to catch the passenger train. In those days, trains would stop in rural areas and get water and pick up passengers. We got to the train station and I was waiting for the train to arrive. The train pulled into the station and steam was coming out from under and around. It scared me and I almost started to run.

Dad laughed at me because he knew it really scared me. He said, "Son, it is okay, don't be scared."

We got on the train and went on to Cedartown to get our supplies. Mom was the only one who drank coffee and a couple pounds would last for months. We raised everything we needed, and salt, pepper, and coffee was about the only thing we had to buy. We never traveled very far because riding in a mule and wagon was very slow.

I would lie in bed at night and I would listen to that freight train try to go up a steep grade close to the relay station. When it was about to rain, you could really hear that train struggling to make it. It would get down very slow and would sound like, "I got to make it, I got to make it, I got to make it," and the engineer would shout, "Throw more coal in we got to have more steam." I would just about give up on it making it when it would start building up some speed. The train would go a few miles, disconnect those box cars, and go back and get the other box cars that it had left and start the process all over again. Glenn said Doc and Shag would go over and for meanness put soap on the tracks and this really made it hard to get over that hill. I bet the train engineer had a few choice words to say.

I looked forward to the day the rolling store would come by. This was our convenience store. The rolling store was a truck with lots of shelves and chicken coops on the back and side of the truck. You could trade chickens and eggs for things on the truck. I would get an RC Cola and a moon pie. After we traded chickens and eggs, the truck driver would drive off. One of our older brothers, Doc or Shag, would hide in the bushes up the road with our favorite mule, Bell. We had a small hill just past where the truck had stopped in front of the house. When he started up the hill, he would go very slowly. One of my older brothers would be on the mule and he would ride up to the back of the truck and steal our chickens back.

Pullen Road went about two miles and dead ended into another road. Those people on the other road did not use the Pullen Road. Dad's number one rule was, "Kids, do not get over on the Pullen farm." They had a big farm and on the left side of the road their land came close to the back of our farm. We would sneak around on this land because it was a long ways from their house. On the right side of the road and about six hundred feet from our house their land started. This area was a no-no and if we got caught, Dad would raise hell with us. We would be hunting on our land close to Luv Pullen's property. We would shoot a rabbits and here Luv would come. He would go to our house and say, "Cliff, was those boy's hunting on my land?" Dad would say, "No, Luv, they were hunting rabbits on my land close to your land."

Luv, his wife Grace, and their two kids, Buddy and Cricket, had a dairy business. They would milk the cows early in the morning. Cresses Pullen, Luv's sister, would take her green pickup truck and go to Lindale delivering milk. Their land was the only land that we could not play on. A couple of times, Grady and I would sneak over on their land and we were very scared. They were strange neighbors.

"Bus" Shiflett—that is what every one called him—lived on the east side of the Pullens. Several years later, one of his cows got out. Luv put it up and told Bus to come get his cow. When he got there, Luv told him he was going to charge him for keeping his cow. They got into an argument and Bus slapped Luv and took his cow home. Later, Bus goes by the Pullen farm, headed to County Line Tavern to get a couple beers. Buddy followed him. Bus went in and got a couple of beers. He came out and got in his car. Buddy walked up and pointed his gun at him. He threw up his arm, and Buddy takes his rifle and shoots his arm off. Bus takes his other good arm and grabs the rifle holding it away from him. My brother Doc was inside and heard the shot and came running out.

He said to Buddy, "Don't kill him. You are going to be in serious trouble." Doc talked him out of shooting Bus again, then he left. Later Buddy was arrested but he beat the charges. It cost him a ton of money to beat it. After that Buddy became very humble. Glenn moved out of the farm and he said, "You could not ask for a better neighbor."

When I lived on the farm, it was very quiet at night and there were only a few families who lived past us. You did not hear any cars going by. The only thing you would hear was whooper wills and maybe an owl hollering at night. Our only night light was if there was a moon out that night. I was not afraid of the dark, I was raised in darkness.

In the fall when the weather turned colder we would butcher a hog and cut the hog up and we'd make our own sausage. We took the hams and rubbed them in lots of salt. Afterward, we would put the hams in a flour sack and hang them in the smokehouse. The salt would keep worms from getting in the meat. We made our own lard by taking the fats from the hog and putting them into a big black cast iron pot. We would build a fire under the pot and boil the meat until it turned into lard. We also killed rabbits and squirrels to eat. We raised our own chickens to eat and we had plenty of fresh eggs. Our hog had a litter of pigs and one of them was very white and he really stood out. Grady and I took a liking to him. As he got older, we would let him out and he would follow us around like a dog. We named him Oscar and he was our favorite pet. You did not let hogs run outside. You kept them in a hog pen. Oscar stayed outside and never bothered anything. But D-Day was approaching and one day Dad carried Oscar down close to the well with a big pine tree close by. That was where they butchered hogs. Grady and I knew what was going to happen and we started crying and we could not stand to watch Oscar being shot. Grady and I could not eat pork for months after that. We learned one thing. You do not make pets out of farm animals you are going to eat because that was the way farm life was.

Mom and my grandmother, Anna Cargle, would take the flour sacks and feed sacks and make quilts for the beds. They would cut small sections out of the sacks sew them together to make a quilt. It seemed like it took weeks to make a quilt. I remember they would order clothing patterns and lay those patterns out on the sewing table and make lots of our clothes with those sacks.

We had cows for fresh milk, not concentrated milk like we have today. There was one job I enjoyed. I'd fill a churn with milk and I would sit there and lift a dasher up and down and make buttermilk. Butter floated to the top and we had fresh butter and buttermilk. Corn bread, onion, and a big glass of buttermilk was one of my favorite meals. We raised lots of fresh vegetables, what would today be called organic. My sisters, Barbara and Jewell, would help Mom take quart jars and can vegetables to help carry us through the winter. Mom would make up a batch of soup, put it in jars, and then put it in this big pot and set it on the stove. The pot had a gauge on it and a place for the steam to come out and I remember it getting too hot and blowing up. Luckily no one got hurt but it made one heck of a mess.

When you wanted a drink of water, we had a water bucket with a dipper to dip water out. The dipper was hung on a nail beside the water bucket. When you got thirsty you would pick up the dipper, put it in the bucket, scoop up a dipperful of water, drink, and hang the dipper back on the nail. Everyone would drink out of the same dipper. There was no cover on the water bucket. When someone got sick, everyone would get sick and I wondered why. Lots of people back then either dipped snuff or chewed tobacco. I hated it when someone would take the dipper scoop up water out of the bucket, wash their mouth out, and put the dipper back in and get another scoop of water and drink it. Back then we did not have drinking glasses. After we used the peanut butter or mayonnaise jar up that was our glasses to drink milk. Also, if they were not available, we used small fruit jars to drink out of.

Dad would not let us hunt quail but if we were hunting rabbits and we came upon a covey of quail we would kill two or three and we would take them home clean them and put them in a pan of lard and cook them. Quail was a delicacy and it was a treat to eat them. Dad would let two bosses at the cotton mill hunt on our farm. Marshall Botts used a 12-gauge Remington and Homer Mathis used a 16-gauge Fox shotgun. They wore very nice hunting jackets with lots of shells on them. I was scared of them because they seemed so rich. Homer brought his young son Jack with them and Jack told me he could not use a gun and his job was to retrieve the birds after they had been killed. According to Jack, the Brannons had the best farm around to hunt quail. Back then, people lived off the land and there were lots of fields and fewer trees. There were no deer, turkeys, coyotes, or other wild animals. Quail are very hard to find today because most of the farm land has grown up with trees.

My friend, Albert "Red" Burkhalter, was a school patrol member and Pepperell School sent them on a trip to Washington, DC, and when Red got back he came over to our house. Red wanted to go down to a wet water stream that only ran during the winter to catch some craw fish. Red said, "While I was in DC, I had eaten some of them and they were very delicious." I was told you could not eat them but they did resemble shrimp which I had never heard of or seen. Red had no idea what he had eaten and thank goodness we did not catch any crawfish or we might have tried to eat them.

Later in life, after Dad got a car, Dad and Mom would take us to Rome once a month. We always parked at the cotton block in downtown Rome. The cotton block got its name because in the old days farmers would bring their cotton to the south end of downtown Rome and sell their cotton. The cotton block was close to where the Etowah and the Oostanaula rivers met to form the Coosa River. Cotton was sold and then loaded on boats and shipped down the Coosa River. For years, when we went to Rome, we never went past the cotton block. There were a lot of hardware and feed stores on the cotton block where farmers could buy things they needed for the farm. If we did not go to Rome, we would go to the Burkhalter store on the Reesburg Road about three miles north. Hoyt Burkhalter ran the store and lived next door. He did not have any watch dogs but if you wandered off into his yard, he had two geese. These two geese were mean and they would run up to you and bite you. I was really scared of them. Burkhalter's store was a small block building and it seemed like he had about anything you needed.

My first long trip when I was very young was going to the Cargle family reunion. It was somewhere close to Trion, Georgia. Mom's maiden name was Cargle. The reunion was held on a big farm with a creek running through it. Trion is approximately thirty to forty miles northwest of Rome. We traveled US 27 North, and I don't remember whose old flatbed T-model truck we were riding in, but there was a good crowd going. US 27 was a narrow, two–lane, crooked road, but at least it was concrete paved and not dirt. The trip seemed so far away. I had never been out of Floyd or Polk County before this trip. At that time it was the longest trip I had ever taken.

My School Years

I started the first grade at Pepperell Elementary School in downtown Lindale, Georgia. Lindale was a mill village and in 1894 Massachusetts Mills of Georgia was born. The mill began operations in 1896. This was one of the first cotton mills built in this area. The mill owned the houses, drugstore, clothing stores, restaurants, shoe shop, grocery stores, service stations, you name it. The company also had a doctor and a dentist office in the village. There was a large auditorium with a movie theater and a pool in the basement. Pepperell Mill produced their own electricity. At first the house had outhouses as toilets. Not many years later, bathrooms were installed inside. When the mill was first built, all roads to the mill were dirt roads. When it rained hard, they had a hard time getting supplies to the mill. The mill built a trolley line going by what is now Darlington School and on to South

Broad Street and on into the Cotton Block. The trolley stopped in early 1930 when roads were paved and trucks started hauling freight.

If you needed to go to Rome, there was a bus service between Rome and Lindale. If you lived in the mill village you had everything you needed. Lindale had their own policemen who patrolled Lindale. The mill paid their salaries. The mill had their own fire department and every Friday at twelve noon the mill would blow the whistle. The firemen would head out, sirens blaring, on a practice run and to the area of the suspected fire. The whistle would blow different signals and this would signal where the fire was located. Pepperell Cotton Mill made blue jeans and overalls. Pepperell would dump their blue waste dye into the creek. The dye turned the creek blue. The creek ran blue for approximately five to six miles before entering the Etowah River. Today the EPA would've put a stop to dumping blue dye into the creek. And they should have put a stop to it. There were at least three cotton mills in the Rome area, and almost every city around had a cotton mill. Today, I do not know of a cotton mill in this area. King cottons days are gone.

Pepperell Elementary was a two-story wood frame building that looked like a three-story building. The ceilings were very high, probably around twelve feet. This was a modern school for its time. We had radiant steam heaters and they were heated by a coal boiler in the basement. We had indoor bathrooms. My sister-in-law, Debbie Priest Gable, went to Felton Grammar School in Felton, Georgia. Felton was a very small town just south of Cedartown and just over in Haralson County. This was where my wife, Barbara S. "Bobbie" Priest, was raised and went to school. Today, Felton has a post office and a fire department and that is about it. When they rebuilt US 27and made it a new four lane, it wiped the town out.

Debbie said when she started the first grade in 1955, the school had outdoor bathrooms for girls to the left and boys to the right. She said they had coal heaters and older boys would keep coal in them. Pepperell Elementary School was very modern for its time, but the building was a fire trap. I believe I was in the second grade when they installed a large metal tube from the second floor to the ground. This was an emergency fire escape. At first they would let us play in the emergency fire escape. We would slide down so much it was wearing the metal tube out and I believe a teacher during fire drills got hurt. End of sliding down the metal fire escape.

We lived on the Pullen Road and had to walk up the hill to Doyle Road around 7:00 a.m. to catch the school bus. I wore blue jeans and my sister Barbara wore overalls. We were the first to get on the bus. The school bus had a small heater close to the bus driver. The heaters main purpose was to keep the bus driver warm. I was cold until the school bus picked up other students. Our bus traveled for miles down the back county dirt roads in the south east of US27 in Floyd county picking up other students. We would be the first on and the last off, usually around 4:30 p.m. For lunch I carried two peanut butter and jelly sandwiches wrapped in clear wax paper and in a brown paper sack. My dad gave me five cents to buy a small Coke. Pepperell Elementary did not have a lunch room but they had a small building behind the school where we could go buy the Coke, sit down, and eat our lunch. We always carried a peanut butter and jelly sandwich because they would not spoil. My first grade teacher was Mrs. Kerr, a very sweet teacher and I really liked her. Now the second grade teacher, Miss Fannie Sproull, looked mean, and she *was* mean. If you ever saw a mean teacher in movies, she could have played the part. If you misbehaved, she would take your hand, open it up, and take a wood ruler and leave you with a red hand or take a large paddle and leave you with a red butt. I was a very good boy and I got a spanking from her. We all were scared of her. After the second grade I had good teachers.

Back on the Farm

We lived a hard life and we were very poor, but we did not realize how poor we were. Remember, almost everyone was poor in those days. Through all of this we lived a happy life. We were very seldom sick. One thing we learned early in life was to watch out for mad dogs.

Dad said, "Son, if you see a strange dog, fox or even one of ours coming your way and it is slobbering at the mouth get away from it as fast as you can. If you think you cannot outrun it, climb a tree."

I was playing with Grady up on Doyle Road just above the house when I saw this big brown dog coming down the road toward us. He was slobbering real bad and walking real slow. Grady and I ran home and told about us seeing a dog slobbering at the mouth. My dad got our shotgun and went up there and killed him.

Glenn said, "One time a mad dog came by and got into a fight with one of our dogs and they shot and killed the mad dog. They tied up our dog to see if he would go mad. The next day they checked on our dog and sure enough he went mad."

Shag, Happy, and Glenn went behind the house where he was tied up. Happy had a pistol and Shag had a shotgun and Happy said, "I am going to shoot him with this pistol." Happy pointed his pistol at the dog, pulled the trigger, and shot at the dog but he missed and shot the rope in two. That made the mad dog madder and he came charging at them. Just in time Shag shot him with the shotgun and killed him. Glen said, "That was one scary moment." If you got bit by a mad dog you had to take lots of painful shots.

In the summer we did not wear shoes. One summer day I was playing with my brother Earl, who was about three years older than me. Earl and I were playing chase in a field in front of the house. I stepped on a piece of glass and cut my foot very bad. Earl carried me back to the house. Mom and Dad wrapped my foot in towels and drove me to McCall Hospital in Rome. I had cut the tendons to my big toes. They put stitches in my tendons and stitches in the cut on the bottom of my foot. Approximately two months later the stitches to my tendons gradually came out of my foot. I walked sideways on my foot for several weeks and it was tough getting around. I don't know why I did not have crutches to get around with. You did not break bottles or jars, and if Dad caught us breaking one, boy, would we have got a bad wiping.

I remember Mom getting very sick. She was laying on her bed hollering and crying and saying, "Call the doctor, I am hurting."

Dad drove over to Highway 27, stopped at a store, called Dr. Cliff Moore, told him, "Grace is very sick." He came right on out and I can remember Mom laying on her bed and Dr. Moore running his stereoscope over her stomach.

After a little while, he turned and said, "Okay, Cliff, go over to the highway and call an ambulance, and I will meet her at the hospital." He went over and called Henry Autury Funeral Home in Lindale. Back then funeral homes had the ambulances and they would load you up and put you in the back and rush you to the hospital. Remember, back then there were no EMTs and you received no medical attention on your trip to the hospital. And if you died on the way to the hospital they would take you to their funeral home. They had to operate on Mom and take her gallbladder out. Mom was bedridden for several weeks. In those days doctors came to your house if you were sick. My, how times have changed.

Christmas was very special. We would cut a small cedar tree bring it home and decorate it. We would take popcorn, run a string through it, then hang it around the tree. We would put small handmade things on the tree. We had no electricity so we had no Christmas lights, but we had a beautiful Christmas tree. For Christmas, my younger brother Grady and I were very excited. We got a Red Ryder wagon for us to share and a bag of oranges, apples, and nuts for everyone to share. The next Christmas we each got a BB gun and I thought I was in hog heaven, plus we got a bag of oranges, apples, and nuts. Today, that doesn't seem like much, but back then that was a big Christmas. My favorite toy I played with was a half-pint whiskey bottle. It was small and flat and I could go fast on my dirt track. Grady and I would play Army, and we would stick sticks in the ground and then back off and throw chunk of dirt at them and this was our war game. We always had something to play with. I learned to swim in the Burkhalter pond. I would take two one-gallon metal whiskey cans which had a spout on them. We put a cork in the spout and then I would tie a string from one spout to the other spout and that was my life preserver. I would lie across the string and swim around the Burkhalter pond. Also this was our bath tub in the summertime.

My brothers Glenn and Earl and cousins Melvin and Daniel Cargle decided to build a homemade boat and put it in the Burkhalter pond. They made Marvin Cargle and I go to US 27 and scrape tar out from in between the joints in the concrete highway. Highways in those days had an expansion joint about every twenty feet and they poured tar in each joint. They carried the boat by hand approximately one mile over to the Burkhalter pond. They put it in the water and yes it leaked. They went swimming and made my cousin Marvin and I go about two miles back over to the highway and get more tar. We brought the tar back and they patched the boat and it floated. This is a pond and not very big, but we had lots of fun on this boat.

I will never forget when our cousin Herman Smith came to live with us. He had been in the Army and he became disabled and they discharged him. Herman received a government check and he could hardly walk and he was not able to do anything. It was not past Herman to call a taxi and take him to Florida. We thought he was rich. Herman had bought a case of homebrew whiskey and he always had me and Grady going to get him some homebrew. They had let the homebrew down into the well to keep it cool.

We had a duck pond that was very small and had very dirty water in it, and I mean dirty water in the front yard. We had two ducks and they would play in this small pond. Herman would always sit in a rocking chair under the big oak tree in our front yard. Herman said, "Roy, Grady, go get me a couple of bottles of homebrew," which we did but we got tired of running back and forth to get his homebrew. We took two empty bottles, went to the duck pond, and we filled them up and it looked just like homebrew. We went over to where Herman was sitting in his chair. He could hardly get around and we handed him the bottles of what he thought was homebrew. He turned one of them up and took a big drink, and I mean a big drink, then all of a sudden started spitting out the dirty duck water and started hollering and screaming "I am going to kill you little ——." If he had caught us, I guess he would've killed us. After that, Herman did not ask us again to keep bringing him homebrew. We never turned our backs on him. I believe we learned that from Shag.

Later we got a young horse called Red and he was a Strawberry Roam and he was a very beautiful and gentle horse. I was sitting on him and Glenn was walking beside Red while I was sitting on him with no saddle. We were walking the horse to the front of the house and when we got to the road in front the house the horse took off running as fast as he could. He was headed to the barn where they would put him up for the night about a quarter of a mile away. I hung on to him for about two hundred to three hundred feet and I was hanging on for as long as I could with no saddle. I was just a small kid and I fell off. Luckily I did not get hurt. When my older brothers would take him back and put him in the pasture for the night and when they got him to the road in front of the house they would make him run as fast as he could back to where they put him up in the pasture for the night. My best friend, Red Burkhalter, loved that horse and he would come over to see me but he really came over to see Red the horse. Red loved this horse and wanted to buy him. At first Dad said no but later gave in. Red rode the horse home and his mother was very scared of the horse and said, "No, you are not going to get that horse."

Red said, "Mom, he is a very gentle horse."

"No, and that is it."

Red was very disappointed that he did not get the horse.

Special Times

When I was in the second grade Georgia Power ran electricity to our house. TVA had already run electric power into northern Floyd County. If it had not been for TVA competition, it would have been years before we had electricity. We were very rural and houses were not very close to each other. Now we could do away with our kerosene lamps. Now all we had to do was pull a string to turn the ceiling lights on. No wood stove now; we had an electric stove to cook on and later a electric water heater. No icebox, we had a refrigerator to keep things cold twenty-four hours a day. Now we had a freezer locker to keep our food in. Bye-bye scrub boards, now we had a washing machine. When you washed a load of clothes you had to hand feed the clothes into a ringer to squeeze out the water. This was dangerous as you could get hurt if you got your hand caught in the ringer.

Now we could get rid of that big battery we used to listen to our radio for only a couple hours a day. Now we could listen to our radio twenty-four hours a day. The *Lone Ranger* was my favorite to listen to. Yes, we finally put a sink in the house but no bathroom. The washing machine stayed outside and we would take a hosepipe and fill up the washing machine. We ran an electric cord outside to run the washing machine and covered it up when it was going to rain. Several weeks later Doc worked for Rome Roofing and Sheetmetal Co. He made a sink and installed it in the kitchen. Also he moved the washing machine to the back porch. We were moving on up. Today, I look back, they were obsolete, but in those days they were very modern. We were moving on up!

Mule Drive

Dad would plow the fields to plant corn and he would hook up a plow to our mule Bell. I would walk beside the plow and I would hold two long straps to guide Bell. When you wanted Bell to move over to the right dad would say "gee" and I would pull the right strap just a little. If dad said "gee gee" I would pull the strap a little harder. If we needed Bell to go left dad would say "haa." Bell was a good, gentle mule and she learned fast. After a few weeks, Dad was the mule driver. He would take the strap and throw them over his shoulder and he would guide the mule with the words "gee" or "haa." If Bell got out of the pasture she would not run away. When she did get out of the pasture you could just walk up to her and lead her back to the pasture. We had two other mules that were totally different like Doc and Shag. When they got out they just kept running and running. It would take at least a half day or longer for at least two or three people to catch up with them. They were on the wild side and we had to herd them back to the farm. When we used these two mules I had to be a mule driver again. They were lucky Dad did not kill them.

Dad finally got a car and I do not remember what kind of car. I remember Dad would always park on a small hill beside the house. To start the car, Dad would let it start rolling down the hill and let the clutch out and the car would start. When Dad went anywhere he would always park on a hill. And there were lots of hills in Floyd County.

Mom and Dad worked in the cotton mill. My oldest sister Sarah and her husband, Jesse La Rue, also worked in the cotton mill and lived in Lindale. We enjoyed going to visit with them. My sister Barbara and Elizabeth were the same age and Elizabeth's sister, Janie, was a few years younger. I loved to visit with them. They had running water and an indoor bathroom. On the farm when we had to go do our thing we had to walk approximately a hundred feet to the outhouse. If it was windy, cold, or raining, you still had to go. Sears and Roebucks mailed out a large catalog every year and it sure came in handy in the outhouse. Now you know why I said they lived in luxury.

New Business

The family decided to go into the chicken business. They built a chicken house and ordered four thousand baby chickens. We had to haul water to the chickens and I was old enough to fill the water buckets. As the chickens drank the water in the pan I would refill the water cans. They would hook up Bell to a sled, and set two fifty-five-gallon drums on the sled, and pull water buckets by hand up out of the well and fill the drums. The well was approximately two hundred feet from the chicken house. Bell would pull the sled to the chicken house and several gallons of water would splash out of the drums. A problem soon developed as the chickens got older. You could not believe how much water chickens could drink. Thank goodness we had electricity. They bought a well pump and ran water to the chicken house. At about the same time, they ran a water line up close to the backdoor of our house. Now I did not have to walk down to the well to get water, I just walked out the back door, turned on a faucet, and there was water. Now we really were moving on up and getting modern.

Just a few days after we received the first load of baby chickens, a severe thunder storm came up. The storm blew one side of the chicken house out. And the storm blew the baby chicks out into the field. The whole family pitched in and we got the baby chickens up during the storm as fast as we could. We put the baby chickens in a safe place in the chicken house. There was rain and lightning, and the wind was blowing. It was a very bad thunderstorm. After the baby chickens were safe, we ran back to the house. Mom and I were the last ones to get in the house. Just as we walked into the back door of the house, the metal roofing and wood boards on our front porch blew off and hit just outside the back door. It had hit where Mom and I had just been a few seconds ago. That was a very close call and it was our lucky day.

The company that delivered the chickens told us they would be back in nine weeks to pick the chickens up and pay us. Today they would say back in six weeks, not nine weeks. The company we bought our chickens from was always several weeks late. And those extra weeks with the chickens eating a lot of chicken feed cut into our profit. The company came back the third time and wanted to bring us a load of chickens. My dad said, "Now we are out of the chicken business." I was glad. Raising chickens was no fun.

Crazy Things

Dad could do some things that made no sense to me. One of his best ones was picking up rocks. Dad would hook up Bell to the sled and we would go into the fields and pick up rocks. Picking up rocks in the fields made sense. The one I will never understand was when we went into the woods, and I mean woods, and pick up rocks. I would ask my brothers, "Why are we doing this?" and they would say, "We don't know why." After a few years, Dad had emphysema from working in the cotton mill and he was not able to do hard work. I will always believe we did things just to keep us busy. We had about three acres of pulp wood-size pine trees on a small hill close to the house. Dad one day said, "Boys, get the crosscut saws, axes, and bow saws, we are going to cut trees down today" Dad carried us to the three acres of pine trees. There was at least ten acres of fields next to these pine trees. These fields have not been planted in years and small trees and bushes had started taking them over. We started cutting the trees down and cutting the limbs off and cutting the trees up into smaller sections. We would throw them into the small ditches. I will never forget when I asked Dad, "Why we are doing this?" He said, "One day I am going to row crop this land." He never did plant a crop and in a few years small trees were growing up on this land again.

While Dad and Mom were working in the mill they saved up some money to remodel the farmhouse. Dad hired Jesse La Rue, my brother-in-law, to do the remodeling. Dad would show Jesse what he wanted him to do that day. The next morning Dad would tell Jesse to change what he had done. He wanted to do it a different way. Next morning a different way. The next morning same thing. And one day it all came to a halt, Dad had ran out of money. The back bedroom was now the open back porch. Yes, that was the room Glenn and Earl slept in. In the wintertime they had so much cover over them they could hardly turn over. When we woke up one morning there was a large snake on the wall just above them.

Dad got our 16-gauge shot gun and told Glen and Earl, "Don't move, there is a snake just above you. I am going to shoot it, don't move, do you understand"?

They said, "Yes, we understand. Shoot it."

It was very cold and they were sleeping with their heads under the cover. Dad shot the snake and killed it. The snake must have come in on the porch to try and stay warm or came out of the loft. Boy was he fooled. I knew I did not want to sleep on the back porch. Also when daybreak came the chickens came up on the back porch. They would wake you up.

Dad was fired from the cotton mill and times were pretty hard. Mom still worked in the cotton mill and she would ride with Pat Pendergrass, who lived close by. He carried several workers to work. Mom sometimes caught the mill bus that came around like a school bus. Mom's cousin, Mr. Broadway, who lived just across the Polk County line, helped get Dad a job at Batty State Hospital in West Rome. This hospital was where they treated the men who had been wounded in the war. The government built a large airport in the Armuchee area and they would fly the wounded in to the airport then transfer them to the hospital. After the war, it was converted to a TB hospital. The airport was later named Russell Field. Dad would walk about a mile over to US 27. Mr. Dixion lived across the road where Doyle Road came to a dead end at US 27. Dad and Mr. Broadway would ride to work with Mr. Dixion. Before this, Mr. Broadway would ride his bicycle from the Polk County line all the way to West Rome, approximately twelve miles. Very seldom would Mr. Dixion take them home after work and only if the weather was severe. In the morning, no matter how bad the weather, Dad would have to walk over to get a ride to work.

Dad raised hay and corn to feed the mules and kept the mules to raise the hay and corn to feed them. When we were working on the farm, Mom would ring the dinner bell when it was time to come and eat lunch. We would sit down at the dinner table and Dad would stand up and he would shovel the food in as fast as he could and he would say, "Okay, okay, boys, eat up, eat up, we got to get back to work." Today, people say I sure eat fast. Yes, I do, but I was trained to eat fast. That big bell served a lot of purpose and it depended on how fast you would ring it. You would ring the bell very fast for a long period of time, which meant emergency and to come home fast. Just a few short rings meant it was time for us to come home. You could hear that bell a long way off. Almost everyone had a bell. Dad never raised a crop that you could sell. Only thing he raised was corn we could eat. Mom and we kids would always plant the garden in the summer. And we had apple trees, pear trees, and we had fresh vegetables. We had fresh food and our food had no chemicals in them.

Larry Brannon, John's son, would come and spend the summer with us. Larry was about one year older than Grady. We would go into the woods and play all day. When we got thirsty we would find a steam of running water and lean over and drink from it. You made sure that it did not run through the cow pasture. We were around eight or nine years old at this time. Mom would say, "I want you kids to be home by 3:00 p.m." We could tell the time of day by looking at shadows from the sun. When there was hardly any shadow it was high noon. Larry, Grady, and I would walk over to the store on the highway to get cold drinks. While we were in the store, someone would ask, "Who is this young lad with you"? Larry would speak up, "I am Larry Brannon and this is my Uncle Grady." Grady was younger and it would make him so mad for Larry to call him Uncle Grady.

Seals Cargle, our mom's brother, would drop Jimmy and Jo Cargle off at our house and he would say, "I got a job up north and I need to leave the boys with you for a few weeks." The weeks usually were a few months. Seals was on the wild side and he had been married at least seven times. Back then you hardly knew anyone who was divorced. And when you would see him he would brag about how much money he was making. Before he left he would hit Dad up for money but Dad never loaned him any. Dad did not have the spare money and he knew he would never get his money back.

About once a week we had to go find a sweet gum bush and break off small limbs off. After we got these sweet gum limbs we would take them home and every one would make them a tooth brush. You would take the end of the stick and chew on it and get it soft. We used Red Diamond snuff as toothpaste. Don't laugh, it worked, and that was all we had. You did not want to go to a dentist because they did not have all the modern things to prevent pain like today. It was very painful to go to a dentist. When they pulled your tooth, they did not give you a shot. They just pulled it out. Glenn went to see Dr. Stegall, the Lindale dentist, and he had a bad tooth in the very back of his mouth. They gave him chloroform which put him to sleep, and then they pulled it.

Cousins

Uncle Gus and Aunt Tench Cargle lived on US 27 about a mile from us. We would go over and play with our cousins Ted, Tommy, and Morris. They were all about the same age as us. Uncle Gus and Aunt Tench would go to bed and let us have the run of the house. We would turn the lights out and team up and have a rubber gun battle. The way you played this game, you would take a piece of wood and cut it out like a pistol. We would attach a clothes pin on the back of the handle and we would take a tire tube that was no good anymore and cut the tire tube up into 1/2 inch strips. I would load my gun by putting the rubber strip over the end of the barrel and stretch it back and locked into place in the clothes pin. If you were lucky and found a red tire tube you could make the gun barrel longer. Red rubber would stretch longer and shoot a long way.

One night we were playing and I was hiding behind a chair in the living room. When playing in a rubber gun battle, you had to shoot very fast to win. I was in the living room and someone stuck their head around the kitchen door and I fired. It was my young cousin David who was about four or five years old. David started crying and Aunt Tench got up and came in there. It scared David more than hurting him and Aunt Tench takes him to bed and I felt very bad about shooting a baby.

Uncle Gus and Aunt Tench one night started telling us about "old bloody bone." They said, "If you are bad, the old bloody bone would get you." They would say, "Listen, listen, I can hear him, he is coming to get you now. Listen, I can hear him, can you hear him hollering?" I actually thought I could hear him and we were all was scared and crying. We went home the next day and told our Mom what happened. Mom would say, "There is no such thing. They are just scaring you kids, don't yawl believe it."

Our cousins really believed it and they were very superstitious. Next time we went over to visit, we would not believe that stuff.

Our other cousins, Melvin, Daniel and Marvin Cargle, lived about two miles over on US 27 north of Uncle Gus. We would walk about two miles through the woods to play with them. There was a big watermelon patch about a mile behind their house. Mr. Miller would not let us get a watermelon to eat. We would go through the woods and one of us would stand as a lookout and watch for Mr. Miller who lived across the street and up the hill. We would run out of the woods, grab a watermelon, and run back in the woods and eat it. Also down the highway lived Mr. Ed Reynolds, and he told us, "Boys, if yawl wanted a watermelon, help yourselves." We would still sneak around and get his watermelons but his watermelons were not as good as Mr. Miller's because Mr. Reynolds took the fun out of borrowing a melon.

Walking through the woods was better than the dirt road. When walking on the dirt road, if a car came by you would get covered in dust if you did not get way off the road. Our house was built very close to the road, about sixty feet from the road. On a very hot, dry day and the wind blowing in the right direction, our house would get covered in dust when a car came by. We had very little grass around our house. The cars would park beside the house and we had a very big oak tree in front of the house. We had a dirt yard. Why that house was built so close to the road I will never understand. I guess when the house was built people used horses and wagons and there were very few cars. It was nice having two sets of cousins living close by. Mary Ellen, Nellie, and Francis Brannon, our aunts, lived next door to our aunt Bessie Cargle.

My grandfather, Ulysses Grant Brannon, was born April 19, 1868, in Floyd County. My grandmother, Mary M. Scott Brannon, was born June, 30 1871. They had seven boys—William, Luther, Ulysses Richard, Clifford Charles, Isom Grant (Todd), and Jack. An infant son and infant daughter died. Mary was injured when a cow stuck its horn in her stomach. She died December 27, 1916. After my grandmother died, my grandfather married Pat Bedford and they had one daughter, Pearl. That marriage did not work out and my grandfather divorced her. He then married Constance Abrams, only eighteen years old, when he was sixty-one. They had four girls and the youngest, Janie Ruth Brannon, died when she was ten days old. My grandfather died May 17, 1940, he was seventy-five years old. Grand Maw Constance raised those three girls and had a very hard time.

Picking Cotton

Our family and Grandma Constance's family would go to our neighbor's farms and pick cotton. You would put a wide strap over your shoulder and pull a large, heavy duty bag behind you. I would go down one row of cotton and pick cotton on both sides of me. The farmers paid two dollars per one hundred pounds. Cotton is light and it takes a lot of cotton just to weigh one pound. I was lucky if I picked twenty-five pounds and made fifty cents a day. Grandma Constance was about 5'5" tall and weighed about a hundred pounds. She could pick more cotton than anybody. She usually made two or three dollars a day. Mary Ellen told me that later on, they would get around $3.50 per hundred pounds. Mary Ellen Said, "her sister Nellie and her mother were two of the fastest cotton pickers around." I knew one thing, I was not a cotton picker.

Cousins Move Away

After a few years, Uncle Gus and his family moved to Norfolk, Virginia. Aunt Bessie and her family moved away. They moved down past Coosa, Georgia, on Highway 20W, about twelve miles west of Rome. The only way we could go visit with them was when one of our older brothers would have to take us. My older brother would take the short route by traveling dirt roads and cross the ferry below Coosa, Georgia. I enjoyed the ride across the Coosa River. When we pulled up to the river and the boat was across the river, we would have to wait until it was pulled over to our side. Shag would pull the car onto the boat and they would pull it very slow back across the river. If we hitchhiked we would have to catch a ride into Rome and then catch a ride to Coosa. This would have been hard to do. They lived across from the Coosa River and we would go swim in the Coosa River. I was just a small kid and I was lucky I did not drown. The Burkhalter pond was a lot different and I was lucky I did not get caught in the current in the Coosa River. Thank goodness they only lived in the Coosa area for a short period of time. They moved to Calhoun Avenue in North Rome.

We got our spending money to go visit with them we would walk over to US 27 and start picking up coke bottles. Glenn, Earl and I would get two sacks and we would head north on US 27. We would walk north on the right hand side picking up Coke bottles and maybe a refundable beer bottle after people had thrown them out of their car windows. You could get a two-cent refund on Coke bottles and five cents on a refundable beer bottle. You were lucky to find a beer bottle. After we walked approximately five miles north to the Six Mile community, we turned around and headed south on the other side. When we got to the County Line Tavern a few hundred feet from the Polk County line, we sold our goods. Polk County was a dry county and you could not buy beer there. After we sold our goods, we walked about a mile home and got ready. We then walked back over to US 27 and hitchhiked a ride to Rome.

Hunting

The only thing to hunt in the late forties and early fifties were rabbits, squirrels, and possums that you could sell. You would have to put possums in a sack and carry them alive to sell. Just one problem, you could not hitchhike a ride with a live possum. Squirrels were too time consuming to hunt. Rabbits were the best choice. The only other thing we could hunt for ourselves was quail and turtle doves. In those days, there were not lots of trees because it was farming country and people lived off the land. Today, lots of trees and no quail but plenty of deer, turkey, beavers, you name it. If we had deer and turkey back, then we would have had plenty of spending money.

In the wintertime, we hunted rabbits to get our spending money. We would get up early Saturday morning, get the dogs, and start hunting. We had one 16-gauge single-barrel shotgun. Glenn could shoot the best so he was the one who used the shotgun. To the best of my memory, shotgun shells back then cost about ten cents each. So if you missed you cut into your profit hunting rabbits. We only got fifty cents for a rabbit and you could not afford to miss. After we killed three or four rabbits, we would carry them home and clean them. You had to leave the hind legs on or you could not sell them. People had sold cats for rabbits. After we cleaned the rabbits we wrapped them in clear wax paper. We then walked over to US 27and hitched a ride to Rome.

If we were let out in the South Rome area, we would walk through the black neighborhoods, usually the Twelfth Street area, and sold our rabbits. After we sold our rabbits, we then walked about three miles to our cousins' house in North Rome. On our next trip to Rome, if we were let out in the North Rome area, we did the same thing. That night we all would walk to downtown Rome, which had at least three movie theaters. For twenty-five cents you could get into the movie and buy a bag of popcorn and a Coke. After the movie we walked back to North Rome. We were poor but we always had plenty of good food on the farm. When at my cousins' house, for breakfast we had either oatmeal or Jell-O. For lunch we had cornbread and pinto beans. For dinner we had cornbread and pinto beans. The only time we had different food was when one of my older brothers carried us. We would take a dozen eggs, a gallon of milk, and sausage with us. I have seen my cousin Marvin take a glass of water and pour

Carnation milk in it and crumble up crackers or corn bread and eat it. This I could not do. We were all poor but at least we had plenty of good fresh food to eat.

While visiting one weekend, it was a very special time in my life. I was invited with Marvin to the neighbor's house next door. I watched my first TV program. I don't remember what program I saw, but I will never forget watching that small TV. It seemed like the TV's screen was about thirteen inches wide and the program was very snowy. I had seen my first TV.

We had cousins on the Brannon side of the family. Uncle Rich and Aunt Beulah Brannon lived in the Rockmart area in Polk County southeast of where we lived. He was a big farmer. He had eight children and we hated it when they came to visit with us. Uncle Rich would talk and it was mostly with Dad. Aunt Beula and Mom would talk and Mom would do 75 percent of the talking. The children would not come out and play and they would just sit and not say anything. Boy, were we glad to see them go home. Then a few years later, Nancy was born and she came into the world talking, and you talk about a talker, she was. We all loved Nancy. Years later, as we all got older and had our Brannon family reunion, we enjoyed being around them and, yes, Nancy could outtalk us. The Brannons were quiet and laid back and easygoing. The Cargles, well, that was a different story and I don't believe there was any quiet Cargle. Most were on the wild side. There were a few exceptions, but very few. I think Doc and Shag had lots of Cargle blood in them.

Hard Times in the South

Dad, Mom, the fourth brother, Charles "Happy," and the second sister, Jewell, all worked in the cotton mill. Happy had a car. In the late 1940s, there were very few jobs. Doc and Shag did not have a job so they worked on the farm and built a liquor steel in a swamp area on the farm. After Coca-Cola made their Coke, they would store it in a wooden drum. They used a drum from the Coca-Cola Company to run their whiskey into. The whiskey in the drum had turned a blue color from the Coke that had settled in the wood. When the liquor was made, the liquor was hot. When it ran into the wood barrel it turned a light blue color. They went to Rome to the Marietta baker and bought some old bread and tried to strain it through the white bread to take the color out of it. It did not work and they threw the loaf bread out in the yard and our dogs ate it. Yes, we had some very drunk dogs staggering around in the front yard. They did not think the dogs would eat the bread. I was too young to remember much about what happened, but I do remember seeing those dogs staggering as they tried to walk. They decided to get some white whiskey to mix with the blue whiskey. After they picked up a load of white whiskey, they were coming down the Reesburg Road when the county police got behind them. Hugh Padgett and his uncle Autry Padgett were plowing a field in front of Burkhalter's store when they saw Doc and Shag coming down the dirt road in an old Desoto. Doc and Shag blew their horn at them and threw their hands up at them. Hugh said, "the old Desoto was running hot and when the dust cleared they saw that the Floyd County Police was chasing them." Autry said, "Let's tie the mules up and go see if they catch the Brannons." Doc turned right on Doyle Road and after going a short distance they would cross a wooden bridge, whereShag could throw the two gallons of whiskey into the creek. The police wouldn't see it because of all the dust. Back then most county roads were dirt roads. Doc said, "There was so much dust coming up behind that old Desoto that I thought if I could keep the car running we could get away."

After they turned off the Reesburg Road, it was just a short distance to that wooden bridge. They had to act fast and Shag jumped into the back of the car. Now he was facing the back of the car. Shag opened the door to his right which only opened halfway and threw the liquor out. Shag threw it out on his right side, but it was the left side of the car and the tow sack got stuck on the wooden bridge. Doc had gotten close to the right side of the bridge so the liquor would definitely go into the creek and not be seen.

Doc let out a few choice words. "Shag —— I told you the right side."

Shag said, "That was my right side."

It was a 4 door Desoto and the left door opened backward straight out and stopped. The right side door would open all the way back and touch the back fender. Shag went left and was not able to throw the liquor into the creek. The police stopped, got the liquor, and continued their chase. About one mile up the road where Short Horn Road ran into the Doyle Road, the old Desoto took its last breath and quit running.

Doc told Shag, "Get out and run."

Shag jumped out and ran up on a bank and just sat down. Doc kept trying to start the car when the police came sliding up behind them. Doc jumped out and started running. Ron Brock, a former Georgia Tech running back, caught up with Shag right off. Clarence Caldwell started chasing Doc. He shot over his head and yelled, "Next time I am going to shoot you."

Doc thought he had gotten away. He glanced around and saw Caldwell about to grab his coat. Doc let his arms go backward and got lose and never slowed down. Caldwell grabbed his coat and came to a complete stop. This gave Doc a head start on Caldwell. When Doc got a head, he stopped, took his shoes off, and put them in a stump hole and got the hell out of there. Back in those days, grownups would go barefoot working on the farm. Shoes were made out of heavy leather and they were hard to run in. Doc ran so hard over Hickory Mountain that when he got way ahead he stopped and threw up because he ran so hard and thought Caldwell was going to shoot and kill him. He listened to see if he could hear anyone running through the woods and he could not hear anything. He headed on over to US 27, and was very sick.

When Hugh got there one of the agents had Shag handcuffed and leaning over the hood of the car. The other agent came walking up out of the woods all scratched up and out of breath, saying, "I almost caught that black man but he stopped, took his shoes off, and he was long gone."

At this time Doc had been working on the farm and had a very dark suntan. Doc walked over to the Haney's house and he got Donald who was dating our sister Jewell to take him home. Doc and Shag were determined to sell that liquor and they got a brown hat and strained their liquor through it. Well, it was not blue, it was a light brown color and they sold it as a charred liquor and made a little profit.

Jim Mahaffe, former county commissioner of Floyd County, said, "Caldwell and Brock was the first county policeman in Floyd County."

Jim Free, a former police chief of Floyd County, said, "Ron Brock was chasing a bootlegger and he wrecked his car and turned it over, The bootlegger delivered his load of liquor about one mile down the road then turned around and came back and helped Ron. That was just the way things were in those days."

Shag got one year probation and that's the story of Happy's car and how he lost it.

I will never forget my trip to Esom Hill, a community east of Cedartown and next to the Alabama line. I was very young and it was in the late forties. I was riding with Doc and Happy when they decided to go to Esom Hill to get a gallon of white whiskey. Esom Hill was a community the police were scared to go into. If you went, you had better have permission to go or know someone. Happy must have known someone over there. We drove down this road and he pulled up to a farm house on the right side of the road.

Happy said, "Every one stay in the car."

A farmer (bootlegger) walked out on the porch and they started talking. Happy went in the house and a few minutes later came out with a gallon of liquor, got in the car, and said, "Let's get out of here." Happy picked a hammer up out of the floor board and said, "If we meet the police on our way out, I am going to bust it." Years later, in the sixties and early seventies, we would get a call to come over and roof a house. I was still scared to go but we had permission and no one bothered us but I was still nervous. My nephew, Willard Brannon, had permission to go over there and his brother Ronald dated a girl from Esom Hill. They could go any time they wanted to. Willard said people would say "Are you not scared to go over there?" and he would say no.

Bootlegging

Due to Dad's health, he was not able to work so he started selling liquor. When I was around ten years old, we would pour liquor up mostly in one-half- or one-pint liquor bottles. Grady and I would take them to a big broom sage field about two hundred feet from the house and hide them. When we got to the broom sage field we would pull up some broom sage and put the liquor bottle in and set the broom sage back in place. In the wintertime, broom sage looked dead and it would blend right in. When Dad had a customer, he would say, "Go get me a half pint and keep a lookout for any one."

Grady and I headed to the broom sage field to the area were we had hid the one-half pints. First, we would walk around to see if anybody was around and there was nowhere for anyone to hide close by because this was a big open field. We would then pull up a stalk of broom sage, grab the liquor, set the stalk back in place, and run as fast as we could back to the house. I don't know how we knew exactly where we hid those liquor bottles but we did. The revenue agents never did bother Dad and I guess they knew he was trying to just feed his kids. Dad had emphysema and was not able to work. Besides, during the late forties, there were very few jobs in the south.

The only jobs were working in cotton mills, stove foundries, or picking cotton. Stove foundries were hot and very hard work. You were lucky if you did have a job in the mills or stove foundry. When young men graduated from school or turned eighteen they had to leave home. Most left and went to Detroit, Michigan. There were lots of jobs in the car factories up there.

To the best of my knowledge, a young attorney general of Georgia, Ellis Arnold, filed a lawsuit against the Interstate Commerce Commission and later he became governor. In the South, products produced and shipped north had a two-dollar-a-ton tax. This was a tax put on the South as punishment for the Civil War. I believe around 1953 this tax was lifted. After this tax was lifted, industries flooded south. Another contributor to the growth in the South was the invention of air conditioning. Today, that two-dollar tax would probably be equal twenty to thirty dollars a ton.

In 1950, my brother Glenn left and went to Detroit, Michigan. Glenn went up there to roof with Doc, Happy, and Donald Haney. After a few years, they left Detroit and moved to Norfolk, Virginia. Norfolk had the largest naval base on the East Coast. There were lots of new subdivisions being developed and there was a great need for roofers.

Cancer the New Year

Today I have kin and friends who died from cancer. I never heard of anyone dying from cancer back then. I am sure people died from cancer but I did not know of anyone. My dad and mom's greatest fear was that we would come down with polio. One of my classmates had polio and it was not a pretty sight. Polio, chickenpox, and measles were of a great concern. I remember I was told, "You go stand under some chickens and if they flew over your head you would not catch the chickenpox." As I said, this was a saying. Today I know this did not work. When I were in the sixth grade they lined us up and gave us a shot and boy did it hurt. And there was lots of crying kids, except me, yeaaa. I don't remember what the shots were supposed to keep you from catching but I believe it was to prevent chickenpox, measles, or whatever. All I do remember was that it really hurt and left a sore on my arm and later a round scar when it got well. If you did not have that scar on your arm, that meant it did not take and you would have to take it over again. You would know the ones who had the shot because it left a round circle scar on their arm. I believe they started giving polio shots in 1954 and now our parents felt a sense of relief.

Moving Away

After I finished the sixth grade at Pepperell Elementary in 1952, we loaded our furniture on a three-quarter-ton pickup truck. The furniture was stacked very high on the pickup truck. The Clampetts were moving to Norfolk, Virginia. We covered the furniture with a tarp and I still don't know how all of that furniture was loaded on that truck. We started the long journey to Norfolk and I think it was about six hundred miles. All I know, it was a very long trip. This country boy had never been over forty miles from home. We arrived in Norfolk and our brothers had already rented an apartment close to downtown. We settled in and a few days later, Grady and I were riding with Doc and he stopped at a restaurant to eat breakfast. I ordered my breakfast and the waiter brought me my breakfast and to my surprise there were hashed brown potatoes on my plate. I had never heard of anyone eating potatoes for breakfast. Welcome to the big city. Living close to downtown Norfolk was neat. I could walk downtown to the movies or go catch the ferry that went over to Portsmouth, Virginia. Once the ferry landed at Portsmouth it was just a short distance downtown and they had lots of movie theaters I could go to. When I used the ferry, I would see lots of different types of ships. Norfolk and Portsmouth were Navy towns. When sailors came into town after a long period of sea duty, it was party time in the city. I saw signs that said "Sailors, keep off the grass." You cannot blame those sailors for having a good time. After being at sea for a long period of time, they deserved it.

Earl and I would walk down to the newspaper office and we would pick up a stack of newspapers and then we would walk downtown, stand on street corners, and start selling. This was how I made my spending money. Later I decided to go big time. I now had a bicycle and I decided to get a paper route. I got the paper route and had lots of customers. Saturday was the day I went around to collect my money. I was out of school and each time I delivered a newspaper I tried to collect my money. Collecting the money was time consuming. They would not be at home or they'd ask me to come back later or that they simply didn't have the money right then. I heard all the excuses. Lots of times I would have to borrow money from Mom to pay for my newspapers. That was a good learning experience for things later in life.

Later we moved into a duplex on Princess Ann Boulevard. Living there was nice. In the summer while school was out, Doc would take Grady with him roofing. Grady was very young and in the fourth grade but he loved going with them. If he was told he could not go he would start crying. We lived just a few blocks from Robert E. Lee School. I started the seventh grade there. I met people from all over the world and there were students from Greece, Lebanon, China, and other countries. I made friends with a twin brother and sister from Greece. The Greeks could speak very little English. They could not understand the teacher very good. I would explain to them what the teacher had said. They could understand this country boy from the south. I would explain to the Greeks what to do and they understood me very well.

Another Great Experience

I saw the big pond for the first time. I went to Virginia Beach and saw the ocean and big waves. At Virginia Beach the waves were so big, and I mean big, and I was too scared to go into the ocean. Later we went to Ocean View and the waves were smaller. I went into the ocean for the first time at Ocean View. Glenn took us to Ocean View to go fishing. My mom was a short woman and she had to put an inner tube around her and she took a cane pole, laid it on the water, and started catching fish. I waded out up to my neck. I laid the cane pole on top of the water. The cane pole would float up and down with the small waves. The small waves would make the cane pole bobble up and down and I caught lots of fish. Everyone in our group caught lots of fish. A man on the beach came up to me and said, "I have never seen nothing like this. I have an expensive rod and reel and I cannot catch anything. You people are catching lots of fish with those cane poles." Today I wonder what people thought about the way we were fishing. I guess they were thinking the hillbillies have arrived. Back then we gave it no thought.

Fresh Water Fishing

Doc and my brother-in-law Donald Haney, married to my sister Jewell, went fishing at Lake Joyce, a freshwater lake. They were out in the lake fishing when the boat motor came off and fell to the bottom of the lake. They had not fastened the motor to the back of the boat very good. The lake was about ten feet deep. Doc and Donald got in their car and went home to get Glenn. Glenn rode back with them to the lake and they got in the boat and paddled out to the spot where they thought the motor had fallen off. Glenn was about eighteen years old and he was a very good swimmer. Glenn said, "When I first dove down into the water, it was so dark. I could not see anything. I felt my way around on the bottom and found nothing." Glenn dove back down and on his third dive, he found the motor. Glenn grabbed the motor and started the slow swim up and he ran out of air and had to drop the motor. Glenn told Doc, "I found the motor and as soon as I bring it to the surface you grab the motor" Glenn went back down, grabbed the motor, and brought it up to the surface. Doc grabbed it. What were the odds of finding that motor in that big lake? I think it was slim to none. Doc and Donald were very lucky to get their motor back.

High School

After I finished eighth grade at Robert E. Lee School, I went to ninth grade at Murray High School. This school was very big with an enrolment of about two thousand students. They offered classes in just about everything. I took music, metal shop, plus regular classes. In my English class, the teacher would ask me questions just to hear me talk and she and every one would laugh at the way I talked. I hated that class and have never liked English classes since. My brother Earl graduated in 1954 from Murray High School. Earl left and went to Rochester, New York, to roof with Doc and Donald. In 1954, Hurricane Hazel, a big, powerful hurricane, hit Virginia. Hazel missed Norfolk but we had high winds and lots of flooding. Buddy Malory, a friend of mine, rode our bicycles around in the storm. We did not want to miss seeing anything. This was my first time to be involved in a hurricane. Tree limbs were falling, roads were flooded, and live electric wires were down and several people died because of those hot wires. Buddy and I were very lucky we did not get killed or hurt. A few months later, Earl moved back to Norfolk with the three-quarter-ton truck. When he was living in Rochester, Hurricane Hazel also came through and a limb fell and knocked a large dent on top of the cab of the truck.

Norfolk was a southern state but was more like a northern city. I have no regrets living in the big city. It was a great experience and I don't ever want to go back.

Back to Georgia

In 1955, Floyd County was growing. GE built a big transformer plant in Rome and Georgia Kraft built a paper mill on the Coosa River west of Rome. Again we loaded all of our furniture on this truck and we moved in 1955 to a duplex on South Broad Street in Rome. We lived only about three blocks from downtown Rome. I went to tenth grade at Rome High School. Glenn had moved back from Norfolk, Virginia, to live with us. Glenn and I got into his 1955 Ford and headed south on US 27 to see our brother Happy, who ran a tavern just north of the Polk county line. Glenn always drove fast and he was going fast down US 27. Just before you got to the tavern, there was a curve and it was not a very sharp curve. In the middle of the curve was a car parked on northbound side of the road and sitting there with its lights on. All of a sudden, Glenn jerked the car hard left and then hard right and came to a screeching stop. Glenn put the car in reverse and went flying backward and came to a screeching stop.

I said, "What are you doing? You are really scaring me."

He said, "Did you not see that man lying across the road?"

I said no, and we got out and ran back to check on him. He had passed out and his feet were touching the edge of the grass and his head almost touching the center line. We got him up and took him down to my brother's tavern and said, "Take care of him" and we left. That was a very lucky man. If anyone else had come along he probably would have been killed. Glenn was a very good driver. We never understood why the people in that parked car did not try to warn us.

In 1956, we moved back to the farm. My older brother Doc left Norfolk and went to California. Doc wrote back and said there was lots of work in Los Angeles. Glenn, Earl, and Dad left for California. Glenn and Earl got jobs in a car factory and Dad went along because he wanted to see the West. After roofing for many years, Glenn had a very dark suntan and everyone thought he was a Mexican. They hated it out there and it took them three months to save up enough money to come back home. Coming back, Glenn said, "We were crossing the desert in Texas when I looked down at the speedometer and I was going 100 mph. I put my hand over the speedometer and I said how fast you think we are going and Dad said about sixty. Then he asked Earl how he things we we're going and he said seventy."

Glenn showed them the speedometer and Dad started hollering, "You better slow down, you had better slow this car down, you are going way too fast."

While they were in California, Mom, Barbara, Grady, and I were living on the farm in the summer of 1956. Jewell came down from Norfolk to visit with us and she stayed about three weeks. The first week she was always telling us to hurry up get this or that done and we just took our time. We thought why be in a hurry when you get through where you are going. Time did not mean anything to us.

After a couple of weeks, Jewell said, "Now I understand why yawl do not get in a hurry."

Living on the farm you are just laidback, totally different from the big city life. When they got back to the farm they started back roofing. They rode around and when they saw a new house being built, they would stop and ask, "Could we roof this house?" They got a lot of nos and a few yeses. They gradually began to build a business and they built the roofing business mainly in the Cedartown area. Glenn was very fast at nailing on shingles. Earl was slower but he nailed the shingles on at a steady pace and in a days' time he nailed on lots of shingles. My brother Happy lived in Cedartown and that was a plus for them.

Back to Pepperell

In 1956, I started the eleventh grade at Pepperell High School. I knew lots of the students there since I had gone to the sixth grade at Pepperell. I played football on the JV team that year and it was my first year to play football. On August 3, 1957, Doc brought bad news. Happy had died. Everyone was crying and Mom passed out from the bad news. It was a very sad time. Happy was just twenty-nine years old and he had a defective heart. He left behind a wife, Thelma, and two young sons, Willard and Ronald.

In late 1957, I got to drive the three-quarter-ton Chevy pickup truck. I had a girlfriend and she lived halfway between my house and my friend Red's house. You don't take a girl on a date in a three-quarter-ton truck with a big dent on the cab. I would go over to her house to date her. Well, that did not last long she found a boyfriend with a car and that was the end of that.

Grady and I went to Cedartown to pick up some roofing material. We had about one ton loaded on the truck and we headed back home to Lindale. We were coming down the Old Cedartown Highway, and as I was going into this curve, the truck just kept going straight. The steering section had broken. I was probably doing about sixty when I went through a fence and with that weight on the truck it took me a long way to get stopped in that wide open field. Just a few hundred feet back was a deep ditch and I was lucky no car was coming and we did not get hurt, just scared very badly. That was our lucky day.

My senior year I moved up to the varsity team. I weighed about 115 pounds. In those days linemen averaged approximately 150 pounds, but we had three or four players that weighed around 200 pounds. They were not fat, they were tall and heavy built, and you hardly saw any fat people. We played Cass High School, a team that hardly ever won a game. Pepperell beat them very bad and seemed like now the score was 60–12 and our coach, Otis Gilbreth, played the first team the whole game. Lots of the players got mad and quit including me but my best friend Albert "Red" Burkhalter talked me out of it. "Red" was our star running back and he was a very good player. I did not expect to play in the close ballgame but runaway games, yes, I expected to play. Later we played another week team and I believe it was Davis High School. During the game I broke loose and ran about twenty-five yards and I was tackled at the one-yard line. The next play

I was given the football and I was tackled hard and I was about six inches scoring a touchdown. Next play the quarterback, Lowell Curry, kept the football and scored easily. I'll always remember how close I came to scouring a touchdown.

A few weeks later we traveled north about sixty miles to play Ellijay High School in Ellijay, Georgia. They were very good and mean and one of our players, Jim Sisson, who had lived there, said, "My cousin Denzel James played on their team and he was at least twenty years old."

When the bus got close to Ellijay, Otis had the bus pull over to the side of the road and stop. He stood up and said, "Put your windows up and don't speak to anyone." Ellijay area was where a lot of moonshine was made. When we got to the football field it was so foggy you could not see across the field. The grass on the football field looked like it had never been cut. When Ellijay had to punt, which was very seldom, the football would get lost in the fog and you had no idea where it was going to land. Sarah Hames played in Pepperell's band and she said, "As our bus was leaving they threw mud at the buses." Mike Ragland also said, "I also was in the band and it was very foggy." Mike said, "I heard that one of our players, I believe it was Ronnie Corntassall, got hit so hard he did not remember the bus ride home."

As expected we were taken a beating and about that time I heard Otis calling my name out, "Brannon, come here." I ran up to him and stood there beside him. I was thinking to myself, *Please don't put me in. I don't want to play in this game Please don't put me in.* Finally after what seemed fifteen minutes, he said, "Brannon, go sit down." You know if he had put me in, this skinny 115-pound kid would have probably went home on a stretcher. I went to the other end of the bench and stayed out of sight the rest of the game. The next year the Georgia High School Association put in new rules and there was an age limit and you could only play four years of high school sports. Ellijay and lots of other schools were no longer powerhouses for many years to come. Mad one game because I did not get to play and happy one game that I did not have to play. That experience was one of my lucky days.

When I started the tenth grade at Pepperell, I had no transportation to get around in. Tuesday night was teen night in Lindale and Red and I would get a ride late in the afternoon to the auditorium in Lindale. The teenagers in the Lindale area would meet at the Lindale auditorium. The auditorium had pool tables and we would just hang out. When it was over, Red and I would get a ride with Sack Melton who lived about a mile south of Lindale. We would get out at his house and walk about five miles to our house. Red lived about a mile from my house and he would get home first. It was not bad when there were two of us walking at night. I would have to walk home by myself through the woods. We had a trail from his house to my house. I was walking alone and it was around midnight and it was scary. Not long after I had left his house and I was walking and all of a sudden a rabbit jumped up in front of me. At first it scared me until I realized what it was. Another time I was walking home and never carried a flashlight. There wasn't much light that night and I was walking close to home and I missed the trail. I was walking through this broom sage field and I walked up on a covey of quail roosting. Quail roost on the ground in a circle and when they flew up they made lots of noise and flew all around me. Now that was one scary moment. One other time I was walking home I decided not to go through that broom sage field. I decided to go through our neighbor's pasture but it would take a little longer. I knew the cows had the pasture pretty well cleaned and no quail would be roosting there. This pasture would be good walking and while walking through the pasture all of a sudden I came upon a bunch of dogs ahead of me and they were big dogs. I picked up a couple of big rocks. Yes, I was scared. As I got closer, they were eating a dead cow. Thank goodness they ignored me and I went around them and that was another scary moment. Several times Red would talk his dad into letting him drive me home but it was only a couple of times that I got a ride home.

Time to Go to Work

I graduated in 1958 from Pepperell High School and I went in business with Glenn and Earl and we started Brannon Brothers Roofing Company Inc. We had a three-quarter-ton pickup truck and a 1955 Ford car. We roofed mostly new houses and sometimes we would tie the ladder under the Ford car to go roof a new house. On one trip we had tied the ladder top close to the manifold and it burned one side of the ladder. We nailed a 1x4 wood strip over the burned area and we roofed the house. From then on we tied the ladder on top of the car. We roofed a lot of new houses, mainly in the Cedartown, Buchannan, and Tallapoosa, areas south of Rome. I was on my way with the crew to roof a house in Haralson County when I stopped at a small grocery store on US 27, approximately five miles south of Cedartown, to get a sixteen-ounce Double Cola to drink. I went in and walked over to this Coke box and opened one end and there was any kind of beer you wanted to drink. I was startled and the gentleman said, "Cokes are in the other Coke box." Polk County was dry and if I had wanted a beer there was no age limit, money was the age limit.

Marvin McClure was one of our main contractors and he built lots of houses, mostly out in the county. These houses were usually hard to find because they were in the back areas of the county. Farmers could get a government 235 loan to build a new house back then. Marvin McClure would give Glenn the directions and then Glenn would give me the directions and by time it got to me, it was not very good. These houses were being built in the middle of nowhere and somehow I always found them.

On October 3, 1958, Earl married Linda Cook from Franklin, Georgia. We could not stand her. You could look at her and she would start crying. It seemed like she just cried all the time. At first they lived with us and that made things worse. Finally they rented a garage apartment and moved to Rome. We loved it now we were rid of that crybaby. As time went by she started teaching school at Midway Elementary south of Rome. And of all things she learned to fly a plane. Earl calls me and he said, "Linda is flying solo to Texas and she will now have her pilot's license." It was not long that she became one of the family and was a lot of fun to be around. Linda retired at age sixty-one and was going to do a lot of traveling. Approximately one year later she died from a brain tumor. It was a very sad time.

When I graduated from high school we moved to North Lindale and we had a two-party telephone line. On March 2, 1960, Earl and I was roofing a big house on Cave Spring Street in Cedartown when we heard ducks flying over in a V shape heading north. We all looked up at them and Earl said, "Look, ducks heading north. That is a sure sign winter is over."

I had started dating Janice Green and she lived about a half mile from Pepperell High School. Around lunchtime, school had been let out early due to the weather. If I was not working I would go pick her up and take her home. On March 3, 1960, it started sleeting about the time I was picking her up. I carried Janice straight home and it was the right thing to do. I thought, *Roy, you had better get home now.* Everything was okay until I crossed the railroad tracks just past the Lindale auditorium. I started up B Street Hill which is about five blocks long and I could not get up that small hill. By the time I got to B Street, the sleet was coming down very hard and the roads were coated. I tried a second time to go up that hill and go home but I could not make it. A friend, I believe it was Bob Baker, came by and said, "Roy, let some air out of your tires or you will never get up that hill." I got out and let about half of the air out. On my third try I just did get over that hill. I did not have very far to travel and it was smooth sailing. When I got home it was sleeting very hard. Later that night, the sleet turned to freezing rain. I did not sleep any that night because the ice built up on the power lines and trees and limbs would break off. It snowed several inches on top of the sleet and ice. When the limbs broke it sounded like a cannon going off. Later that night we lost power and we had no power for eleven days and the temperature dropped to around zero and did not get above freezing for several days.

The next day I walked about three blocks to a service station and while I was in there an Atlanta Gas employee stopped and came in and told Baldy Staggers, the owner, to cut the gas heat off and if we came back by and it was on they would take the gas meter out. Baldy lived behind us so he could walk to his business. They had no power so they could not pump gas. You could not find gas because there were very few service stations that had power. Finally after a few days, Baldy and Albert Branton, his partner, rigged up a hand pump and now they had gas. Pumping by hand was a slow way of getting gas out but it was better than nothing. We heated our house with radiant gas heaters and we stayed warm. Mom cooked our meals over that gas heater. Several neighbors would come over and cook their food over our gas heater. The heater had a light blue flame because I heard the gas company had to mix propane gas in with their gas so people could have heat. My understanding was all business could not use natural gas because there was not enough natural gas for the business.

About three days later, Grady and I got his1952 Chevy and we went to Lindale. The main road through Lindale had trees, tree limbs, and power lines all over the street. Only one car at a time could travel through Lindale and if you saw a car coming, which was rare, you would have to find a place to pull over because only one car at a time could go through.

We took two eight-foot 2x4s and cut the ends on the front section at an angle. We then cut several two-foot sections of 1x6 and nailed them across the 2x4. We now had a three-man sled and we found a good hill close by to slide down. One day Grady and some friends and I were having a good time sliding down the hill. John Kendrick, about five years old, was standing beside where we would be sliding down the hill. All of a sudden John ran out in front us and we just missed him by inches. If we had hit him it would have killed him and that would have been the end of our sledding.

Contractors now could get in touch with us and at this time we did very little roofing in Floyd County. Our big break came in 1961 when a major hailstorm hit Calhoun and Gordon County just north of Rome. All the roofers left Rome and Floyd County and went north to roof the houses damaged by the hail storm. We had no name recognition in that area. We had a very hard time getting roofing jobs. The local contractors started calling us. Our business took off and when the local roofers came back, they told the contractors they were back and ready to start back roofing for them again. The contractors told them, "Sorry, when we needed you to do our roofs and you were not here so we have replaced you with Brannon Brothers Roofing and they will be doing our roofing from now on."

In those days, if a homeowner needed a new roof, they would call a building contractor to do their roofs. The contractors would call us and we would give the contractor an estimate. In a few years we had developed a very good reputation and homeowners began to call us.

Another thing, we believed in advertisement and we had signs put on our trucks. In the fall of 1961, Grady was playing basketball and during this time he married Brenda Garrett. Grady was no longer eligible to play basketball because if you were married you could not play sports. In 1962, Grady graduated from high school and he was now on board with us and now we had four brothers in the roofing business.

We would split up into two crews, three men in each crew, and we would roof two new houses and then we would meet around 5:00 p.m. to roof the third house. The carpenters would leave at 4:30 and each crew would take one side and we would race to see who would finish first. Back then most new houses were ranch style and low pitch. It would take the two crews working together approximately two hours to roof the house. And in the morning the carpenters would come back to work and they could not believe that the house had a new roof. When we roofed their next house and they were there working, they would ask us how we did it. We had developed a very good reputation and we were able to get the roofing jobs done fast and our customers loved it. Our customers would tell people, "If you want a new roof, get Brannon Brothers. They will do a good job and get in and get out fast" We were the talk of the town. When you first start out roofing you make lots of mistakes. We tore the roof off a house on the east side of Cedartown and the owner stood up on the roof with us and if a piece of decking even looked bad, he would say, "Patch it." We patched a lot of decking on that old house.

Glenn went to collect and he said, "This is what you owe us for patching the decking."

The owner said, "I am not paying for the decking repairs, I am only going to pay for the price you gave me to do the roofing."

Glen said, "This was an extra cost we did not know how much decking was bad."

"Sorry, you should have put it on your estimate that decking was an extra cost."

From then on, all estimates had extra for decking repair. Also we went up to a house to start roofing and unloaded our material, put our ladders up, and was just about start tearing the roof off when the owner came out and said, "What are you doing?"

Earl said, "We are here to roof your house."

The owner said, "I have not authorized any one to roof my house. What address are you supposed to be at?" Earl told him and he said, "That's the house next door."

Back then houses were not numbered very well. We still had not learned our lesson. A few months later we roofed the wrong house and the owner came home from work and wanted to know what was going on. We talked to him and found out again we were on the wrong house, but guess what, he paid us anyway because he was going to have a new roof put on. After that, no more wrong roofs. We made sure if it was the right house. If the homeowner was not at home, we went next door or however many houses it took to find out for sure if we were at the right house. Not long after that, Nath McClinic, who was the first black Floyd County policeman, called Glenn and said, "I want a new roof on my house" and he gave Glenn the address of his house and he told Glenn, "I know you will treat me right."

Glenn said, "Yes, we will and we get it in a couple days."

We went over and roofed his house and there was nobody at home. Later that night, Nath called Glenn and said, "Glenn, why did you roof that white guy's house next door"

"Nath, you are kidding."

"No, I am not kidding, and I never thought you would be prejudiced and not roof a black man's house."

Glenn said, "I can't believe we roofed the wrong house. I'll be over there in just a little while."

Nath started laughing and said, "You roofed my house."

Glenn said, "Nath, you have had it, when I see you."

It had been just a few weeks back that we had roofed the wrong house.

After several years of roofing, Glenn and Earl had different ideas about how to run the company. Earl left and went to law school and became an attorney. Now there were just three brothers left. Brannon Brothers Roofing by this time was the largest roofing company in northwest Georgia. Later we bought a lift truck. Lift trucks were first used by airports to lift things up and unload into airplanes. We would pull up to a house that we were going to roof and we would back up to the house, lift the truck bed up to the edge of the roof, and unload the roofing material. People would ride by very slow and just look at us. Again we were the talk of the town. We stayed together until 1999.

Family Life

After high school, Albert "Red," my best friend in high school, married his beautiful high school sweetheart, Sarah Hames. They had three children: two boys, Tim and Mike, and one girl, Terri. Red is a very successful attorney and Sarah worked for thirty years at Floyd College. Tim became the sheriff of Floyd County, Mike the plant manager of a local firm, and Terrie a successful attorney and now a retired juvenile court judge. Terri is married to Harry Pierce, a very successful businessman.

In 1961, I met Mary McKellduff at the West Rome Church of Christ on Shorter Avenue. My friend John Mills met Mary Evans and after church we walked a couple blocks down from the church to the Dairy Queen. The girls lived close to the Dairy Queen. John got a date with his girlfriend Mary Evans and he told me Mary could not go unless my

Mary could go. To help John, I asked Mary for a date and she said okay. That Friday night, John and I went on a date with our girls.

While I was on my date, I asked Mary, "How old are you?"

"Fourteen, but soon I'll be fifteen."

I said to myself, *Last date, she is too young for me*. After a few days, John called me and wanted me to go double date again. I said, "John, Mary is way too young for me and the answer is no."

John said, "If you don't go, I can't go out with my girlfriend."

I gave in and said, "For you, okay, but this is my last date with Mary."

Next Friday, same thing, I gave in, and next Friday, same thing. After a few months John and his girlfriend broke up. Mary and I had been dating for about a year and I carried her home after our date. We were sitting on her front porch talking and she sits down in my lap and we thought nothing of it. Her dad looks out of the window and saw us, but he did not say anything that night to us. Mary calls me the next day and told me her dad saw her sitting in my lap and that she could not see me anymore. She said, "I am not going to stop seeing you." She would leave with a friend of hers and we would see each other but this got old. We decided to get married and I asked Shag and Helen to go with us to Buchanan, Georgia, and if they would be her parents. Shag loved the idea and they went with us. In those days if you wanted to get married fast you went to Buchanan. It was the place to go. We all went down and went in to the see the judge but he did not buy our story that Shag and Helen was Mary's mom and dad.

Well, I am not the type to give up and a few weeks later we were roofing one of the Polk County judges house. I told him I was thinking about getting married and I asked him what I needed to do. He told me to come by his office and he will give me a marriage license which I can take home and fill out and bring back to him. A few days later I went by and got them and took them home and Mary was now eighteen years old and she signed her dad's signature. I carried them back to the judge. He signed them and said, "You are now ready to get married. Congratulations."

A few days later we went to Rockmart and got a preacher I knew and he married us. After we got married, I called my brother John who lived in Jackson, South Carolina, just outside of Augusta, Georgia. He had a small guest house behind his house and I thought it would be a good place to hide out. John said, "Come on down," and we did. While I was down there, I called her dad and he threatened to kill me. "If you harm my baby daughter, I will kill you." Later we went back to Rome and we got along great. Mary and I moved into a four-room wood frame house on the Cave Spring Road south of Rome. This house was like a shoe box living room and kitchen on the left, two bedrooms and bath on the right. Mary got pregnant and for three months she could not eat anything. She threw up constantly and it seemed like twenty-four hours a day. I don't remember how many times I had to carry her to Floyd Hospital to have fluids put in her body.

Shag moved to a house in front of us. April, 1963 Shag had married Miss Helen Jacks and she had two daughters: Kanita, who was about twelve years old, and Rickey, who was about five years old. Kanita and Shag did not get along very good. We all loved Rickey, she could get along with anybody. Shag loved that girl very much and years later Rickey had two beautiful girls, Penny and Crystal, and Shag loved them very much. They were Pa Pa Shag's girls.

About two years later, on October 10, 1963, we had our first son, Kenneth Roy "Sam" Brannon. Approximately one year later, on December 4, 1964, Steven Craig Brannon was born, and twelve years later, in October 29, 1976, Joel Mark Brannon was born.

In 1966, my number one sister Sarah and her husband Jessie moved to Tucson, Arizona. In 1968, they came home during Christmas to visit. Jessie told Dayton, my younger sister Barbara's husband, that he could make some good money driving trucks in the copper mines. Jessie and Sarah left and went back home. A few days later Dayton packed his clothes and he had fifty dollars and he headed west. Later, Barbara and their two sons—Terry, who was two years old, and Craig, who was six months old—headed west. We seldom ever saw them because it's a long ways to Tucson.

Before we had Joel, Sam and Steve were old enough so we could go places and we were not tied down with kids. Sam and

Steve were always spending nights with friends and kinfolks. Mary had a birth-control device and she could not have kids. Mary did not tell me that one day she decided she wanted to have another baby. She had the device taken out. One evening I came home from work and I could feel something was not right. I said to Mary, "Have you had your period"? And she said no. I told her, "Go see a doctor tomorrow, I want to know if you are pregnant." I slept very little that night and the next day she came by the job where I was working and gave me the news. Grady heard about it and he rushed over to where I was working because he thought I would leave the roof unfinished. Yes, everybody in Lindale knew about it before I did and I was the last to know. Yes, that night I went off with a couple of my friends and I had maybe one, maybe two, and maybe three drinks and then I lost count.

Raising Kids

Raising kids was a challenge because each one of our children had a different personality. Sam was very picky about his food. When Mary cooked breakfast, she would fix Sam toast and he would not eat it if it had the crust on it. She would break off the crust and if you broke the toast he would not eat it. When she cooked his eggs, and took them out of the skillet and broke the yellow, he would not eat it. Only way he would eat a hamburger was plain and if they put mustard on by mistake and I wiped it off, he still would not eat it. He was a very picky young man and I would get very mad at him.

When Steve did something wrong and deserved a spanking and on one occasion I was spanking him and when I got through he said, "That did not hurt." I said, "I bet this will," and I spanked him much harder and he turned looked up at me and said, "Yep, that hurt," but he never did cry.

Another time Sam and Steve had misbehaved and Mary said, "when your dad gets home I am going to have him give yawl a spanking." When I got home Mary told me what they had done and she said, "Spank them." I said, "Okay, come here, Steve, you know you are going to get a spanking," and he said yes. Steve thought I was going to whoop him with a belt so he had put a plate in his pants and I spanked him pretty hard and I almost broke my hand. Now Sam was a different story. When I picked up the belt and on the first lick you would have thought I was killing him. Steve very seldom cried and Sam never stopped crying and hollering. Sam at home would always complain, be stubborn, and kept giving us a hard time. Steve was easygoing and hardly ever gave us any problems.

One day I met one of Sam's teachers and I said, "I bet Sam gives you a hard time in school," and to my surprise, she said, "Sam is a very sweet boy and I wish I had more like him." I was very surprised and shocked. Now Steve was a different story, good at home but very mischievous at school (like Shag). Steve was always bringing home notes from the teachers. Steve would make noises just like a cricket and other animals while he was in class.

While the children were outside playing, Mary and I would decide to have some private time. We would go into our bed room lock the door and about that time Sam would knock on the door and say, "Let me in."

"Sam, go away we are trying to take a nap."

"But, Daddy, I need to come in now."

Sam would not stop until you let him in. A few weeks later I would think, *Well, they are outside playing hard*, so I locked the door. Guess who's knocking at the door and hollering at the wrong time?

When Sam turned sixteen, he had to have his driver's license and a few months later got a ticket doing a hundred miles per hour and a few weeks later a ticket for ninety miles per hour. Yes, he lost his driver's license and my insurance agent Sue Jones heard about what happened and said I had better get him off my insurance or the state would be after me and send for my tag. And if I had not taken him off my insurance, I would have had to surrender my car tag to the state of Georgia. A few months later, I get that letter and I had to prove that he was not on my insurance. Today Sam is totally different. He will eat about anything and very settled down.

Steve was a different story I had to make him go get his driver license at age eighteen and he was always settled down.

Joel was a lot like Steve and easygoing. Joel loved music and started playing in Pepperell's high school band in the eighth grade. Joel's first year in the band and while playing in the eighth grade at Pepperell High School who goes on to win their first class AA state champion ship. Joel played the trumpet and after a few years played a solo on his trumpets during the halftime show. After Joel graduated, he went to Jacksonville State to play with the Marching Southerners.

Again he played solos on his trumpet. Joel was very excited when the Marching Southerners were invited in 1996 to perform in the Macy's Day parade. The weather was very cold and the temperature was around thirty-five and they stood in their starting point for four hours. For a few seconds Joel was highlighted on national TV. Joel was very cold but he really enjoyed this moment.

Good Foods

Mary and I and the boys were headed to the mountains and I had a sore spot on the end of my tongue and I could not eat anything. I stopped at a small grocery store to buy some soup because I thought it would be the only thing I could eat. Also I bought some raisins and I forced myself to eat them and it was hard to do. About one hour later I could eat anything I wanted. I had heard that raisins were very good for mouth sores. Raisins were the right food to eat. Later on we took a trip to Daytona Beach, Florida. My arthritis was giving me problems and I picked up a magazine and read an article that said fried foods will flare up your arthritis. I loved fried chicken, it was my favorite food, I could eat it for breakfast. After that, I cut back on fried foods and my arthritis got better. I remember when I was young my mom would go to Cave Spring, Georgia, to see a doctor about her arthritis.

The doctor would give her pills which did not do any good. Back then everybody would eat lots of fried food cooked in lard. Pills do not cure you; they only help temporarily in my opinion. It was years later I read about fried foods and I had to give up eating lots of fried foods. That was when I started looking and reading about good health. Remember, you must lead yourself to good health.

Things that Happened to Me

Mary and I went to Las Vegas and we stayed at Bally's Casino. I had played slots very late that night and the next morning I got up early and went down to play cards. I was tired and had slept very little and when you're in Las Vegas you do not sleep. After playing cards for a while I had to go to the bathroom which was located just across the hall. There was just one wall that separated the men and the women's bathroom, the men was to the left of the wall and the women's was to the right and naturally I took a right. When I walked in there was no one in the bath room I walked into the first stall and sat down and done my thing. As I got up to put my shirt in my pants, all of a sudden I heard women's voices. Oh no! I was in the women's bathroom. I peeped out the door and saw women at the sink washing their hands. I looked down and saw my shoes and I jumped up on the commode so they would not see my men's shoes. I was very nervous and thinking I was going to be arrested for being a peeping tom. Finally it got very quiet, I could not hear anything so I decided to open the door and get out of there. And to my surprise, there was a lady cleaning the bathroom and she threw her hands up and started screaming. I just kept walking and said, "I went into the wrong bathroom," and I kept walking out. As I was walking out, a lady was going out also. I said, "Ma'am, I'm so sorry that I went into the lady's restroom by mistake." She said, "You don't have to apologize to me, yesterday I went into the men's restrooms." That made me feel a lot better. Today I look at the signs on restrooms. I very seldom go to the right side.

I went to an auction of lots for sale on the Old Rockmart Road in Silver Creek, Georgia. I picked out a good level lot and I paid about three hundred dollars for it. It was a bargain and I decided to build us a new home. I hired a surveyor to survey the lot and was I in for a big surprise. The level lot I thought I had bought was up on a bank and not level. The surveyor said they just walked off the lots and stuck up a marker. Instead of a ranch style house I had planned to build I had to build a split level house. I built my first new house on the old Rockmart Road in Silver Creek, Georgia. We were ready to move in and Grady and Brenda and their kids Jeff and Jill were there. Also our friends Donna Locklear with her kids was there. I had contracted for the house to be built. I was ready for final inspection and we could move in. We only needed a small door to go under the house. Grady was helping me build the small door. Kids were playing and we were installing the door when we heard the skill saw come on and Sam screaming. I turned around Sam had cut his leg very bad. I grabbed him up and ran with Sam to our friend's car because she had our cars blocked in. I held Sam and Grady drove us to Floyd Hospital. We were lucky Sam did not bleed a lot. It looked like he cut a slice of meat off the front of his leg just below his waist. I carried him to the emergency room and laid him on the table. The nurse laid a sheet over his leg and soon Dr. Culbreth, our family doctor, came in and pulled the sheet back and he let out a few choice words.

I asked, with my voice trembling, "Doctor, is it bad? Is it bad?

He said, "You're dam right it's bad, and we're going to take him right now to do surgery on him."

By this time Mary and the rest had arrived. We knew it must be real bad and we were all crying. That was a long wait for him to come out of surgery and we all were very nervous. Finally he came to give us the news. Dr. Culbreth said, "I have good news. Sam is going to be okay." When he first saw Sam he thought he had cut his tendons and would not be able to use that leg again and he would've been a cripple the rest of his life. The cut was very close to his tendons. Sam was a very lucky boy. Sam was about four or five years old when this happened.

While we were living on the old Rockmart Road we were going Sunday to the Brannon family reunion. That Saturday night a lot of my brothers and family gathered at my house. Shag was telling the story of when he got caught at the Georgian Tavern just south of Rome on US 27. We were all gathered around my dining room table and Shag started telling his story.

Shag said, "Swannee, I was at home getting ready to meet this broad from Cedartown at the Georgian. And I dressed up and took me a tie and hid it in my side coat pocket. I told Miss Helen, I am going to play poker. I left, went to the Georgian, told the cod out front behind the bar, and I said, 'Cod, if you see a big Indian come in warn me.' Well, I put that tie on and tied me a big harbor knot and I was out on the dance floor dancing with this broad from Cedartown. We were dancing to the harbor lights when all of a sudden someone tapped me on the shoulder and this broad from Cedartown asked, 'Shag, do you know her?' I said, 'Yes, babe, I got papers on this one.' About that time, Miss Helen grabbed that nice tie and jerked it as hard as she could."

Now, Miss Helen was part Indian, over six feet tall and a big built woman. Shag said, "If it had not been for this old buddy of mine, who had a sharp pocket knife and cut that tie off, the old Suwanee would not be here today."

We all got to laughing so hard my stomach was hurting and Miss Helen fell backward in her chair and hit the floor and the first thing she did was hold up a liquor glass and she said, "Shag, I didn't spill the Crown." Shag was a big Royal Crown drinker. That was a night I'll never forget.

One Saturday night, all of our brothers, our kids, and family went to the Old Mill restaurant just south of Cedartown to eat. We had a large group and they put us upstairs in a large dining room. Doc, when he's drinking, becomes very rude and mean. Doc was very rude to our server and my son, Sam, told me later he would not eat his meal because Doc was so rude and he thought that server will get even and no telling what he would put in our food. Doc stopped the server and was giving the server a very hard time.

I said, "Doc, why are you acting like this? Leave him alone."

"To hell with him." He gave him few more choice words. The waiter shook it off and went on about his business. There is no telling what he put in Doc's food or ours. A few months later, Shag, Helen, Mary, and I went back down to the Old Mill to eat. We had a very good meal and left. Shag called later and he said, "On my way home I got very sick." We had the same server Doc was rude to. I wonder if he thought Shag was Doc. Because the way Doc acted, we had no more Saturday night dinners.

Shag and Doc were welders and members of the Local 76 Plumbers and Steamfitters Union Rome, Georgia, and they traveled all over the USA working. Doc and Shag would always back a renegade for Business Agent (BA). If you backed the BA who won the election, you would get the local jobs. If you backed the loser you had to travel. Doc and Shag always backed the loser and did they travel. Doc has been in every state except Rhode Island and Shag was not far behind.

They were always fussing with other union members. One night at a union meeting Shag was making a lot of noise and Doc pulls out his pistol and shoots about three times into the ceiling. Now that got some people's attention. People would ask us, "Are you Doc and Shag's brothers" and we would say, "No, they are our first cousins."

Two men got in a big argument over if they were cousins or brothers. Mack said, "I know they are cousins because I asked Grady if they were his brothers and Grady said, 'They are our cousins.'"

Alfred, the other guy, said, "I have known the Brannons for years and they are brothers." I don't know who won that argument but I was pulling for Mack. There is one thing I knew, when people asked if they were our brothers, I said cousin and I meant it. Grady and Brenda's big night was on the weekends. Brenda said her sister Sue and her husband Jo Jo would come over on the weekends and they would call Shag and each one would get on a phone and listen to Shag and they would laugh at the stories he told. Shag was their entertainment on the weekends. We had a softball team called Brannon Bros. The first few years we were the worst team in our league. As time went by we got better each year. I was the manager of the team. Gene English, our cousin, moved from Murphy, North Carolina. We hired him to work with us. He was fast and very quick and I put him at shortstop. Perry Baker played first, Kerry Broadway second, Gene shortstop, Yoga Bohannon third, Rickey Stevens left field, Leslie "Bohog" Baker center, and Michel Jonson right. They had built a new softball field on Vaughn Road in Rome. This field only had an outfield fence. I came up to the field and Doc was circling the bases in his car. I pull up and he pulled up beside me and said, "How did you like that for a grand entrance, cod?"

I said, "Doc, you can get in serious trouble for that."

Bohog was the fastest player on our team and he batted left handed. It did not matter where he hit the ball, and if they did not make a perfect play he was safe. His eyes were messed up and if he looked at you he was really looking at a different direction. Lots of time he ran into the first basement. They thought he was going a different direction. I had developed a winning team. At the end of the season we had one game left. AAA Tire was one game ahead of us. If we won we would be tied and we would have to play again to see who the champs would be. We beat them and it was a close game and a hot day. We were going to take a thirty-minute break and play for the championship. Both teams took a break and laid around to rest. After about ten minutes, I said, "All right, everyone get up and let's start practicing." I had learned if you took a long break when working everyone was stiff and did not work well. We got up and started light practicing. The other team looked at us like we were crazy. We started playing the second game and it was no contest. The other team moved in slow motion. We won the championship and beat them very bad.

Shag was at the Waffle House on Shorter Avenue eating dinner when he got into a cuss fight with two other union members and the manager called the police. When the police got there they were friends of the two union members and they beat the hell out of Shag. He wound up in Floyd Hospital for several days. Shag hired Bobby Lee Cook, the best lawyer around and they took pictures of him and I remember seeing them and he looked awful. This happened in the seventies and they sued the City of Rome for $100,000. Everything looked good for Shag to win, but as Shag's luck went, it took a different turn. Shag had been over toward Cartersville playing poker and he was coming home. Yes, he had been drinking Crown pretty heavy and police were working a wreck on Turner McCall Boulevard as you come into Rome and Shag ran into them. He hit one of the policemen with his car and his body left his body imprint in the side of the police car. He was very lucky it only bruised him and he was okay. They arrested Shag and took him to jail and threw the book at him. He was in a lot of trouble but Bobby Lee Cook stepped in and all charges were dropped, plus his law suit was dropped. A few years later I met the policeman who Shag had hit, George Fricks, a good friend of my nephew, Donnie Canada. We got to talking about that wreck and he said, "I have always wondered what happened why they dropped those charges." They told him they were dropping all charges against Shag and for him to keep his mouth shut. I told him

Shag had a big lawsuit against the city. He said, "Now I know why they dropped all charges."

Bud Freeman a very good friend who lived in Wax, Georgia, about six miles east of where we lived. He owned a small store at the corner of Wax Road and Harmony Road. Just past his store was a big lake and Bud owned a strip of land approximately two hundred feet by eight hundred feet on the Harmony Road that went up to the back property of Wax Lake. Bud said, "Why don't you sell your house on that dangerous road and move to Wax." I thought about it. The Old Rockmart Road we lived on had lots of cars that traveled it and it was very dangerous and the children were very young. I sold my house and bought the land and built a nice home about three hundred feet off the road. It was a lot different living way off from the main road. It was very quiet and peaceful and we enjoyed it. Mary's dad, Taylor McKelduff, lived with us. He drew about three hundred dollars per month on Social Security. Taylor and I got along great except when he got his check. He would call a taxi and go to Rome and buy lots of beer and liquor and come home and hide it. Taylor would stay drunk for about two weeks and he was a pain in the ass. One time he had been so drunk and he had run out of anything to drink and he was trembling very badly. I said, "Here, Taylor, drink this coffee to help you sober up."

He was shaking so bad he could not drink it. I went to Rome and got him a pint of liquor and let him drink some of it and he stopped trembling. We could not keep aspirin, Tylenol, or any other kind of medicine. He would take a bottle of Tylenol up in about two days. I could not have shaving lotion, he would drink it. He smoked two packs of short Camel cigarettes a day. Later I was in my bedroom and it was about a hundred degrees outside and I looked out the back window. Taylor was out in our field behind the house. He had his walking cane and he was using it to try and find beer he hid in the weeds. He finally found one and he reached down and picked up a king-size can of Schlitz beer. He opened that hot beer and it shot about ten to fifteen feet in the air and he was trying to put his mouth over the can and drink it. When it was over he was covered in beer. Taylor abused his body and he lived to be seventy-eight years old. He was one of a kind.

Roofing Big Time

In 1974, the new Riverbend Mall was being built in the East Rome area next to the Etowah River. This was our first big roofing job that we had ever done. In 1973, we had just gone through a very good economic boom, but things had started to slow down. When you ordered roofing material it usually took months to get the material. Glenn ordered our material and now you could get it within weeks. We filled our warehouse with roofing material. Glenn put a bid in on the roof of the new Riverbend Mall. We realized that the economic boom was slowing down. If the mall went under it would've taken us down. Glenn put in the contract that if we were not paid within ten days after we turned in our invoice each month for work in progress we would walk off the job. We heard from other subcontractors about their sad stories of how they could not get paid on time and times were getting bad. And sure enough, we did not get paid and we walked off the job. A few days later, they found the money to pay us. Before this roofing job, we had more work than we could do. If you bid a roofing job, odds were that you would get the roofing job and so we did not bid a lot of roofing jobs. I remember that a new Hardee Restaurant was being built very close to Floyd Hospital and the contractor called Glenn to get a price. At first Glenn was going to give a high price and somehow work it into our schedule. Glenn met with the contractor and told him he was going to give him a high price but he decided that was not the right thing to do and Glenn recommended a few small-time roofers that he might be able to get. We worked seven days a week trying to keep up with our roofing jobs. Majority of our workers did not work after Thursday and when they quit for the day they would say, "Meet me Monday morning," and laugh at us and we had no choice but to take it because you could not replace them. They had an opportunity to work and make some good money because we paid time and a half over forty hours. They would only work about thirty to forty hours a week. Then one day the party was over. The economic boom came to an end. We had to lay off 75 percent of our employees. I never will forget one of our employees, Eddie, saying, "What has happened? All I had to do was walk across the street and you had a job." That was a good lesson we learned because what goes up comes down!

Amway Days

In the late seventies, a friend, Gary William, came by my house and said, "I got a business I want to show you." He pulled out a piece of paper and showed me the Amway plan. He was not professional about it. I thought about it and said, "How do I get started?"

He said, "I will get you a kit in a few days and get you started." A few days later I got my kit and I read all the information. I would set my easel, stand up beside it, and practice showing the plan. I wanted to do it right. After a lot of practice I thought I was ready. I called a friend and I said, "I got a business I want to show you and invite some friends over. I will be there at eight Thursday night."

I went over expecting two or three people and I walk in and to my surprise, there was a roomful of people. I was already nervous, now I am really nervous. I had never stood before people and given a talk. They knew I was nervous and I stumbled through the plan. When I finished no one hung around to ask questions. They were all anxious to get out of there and I was just as anxious to get out. I blew a good opportunity to get people in my business. Next I showed the plan to couples and one on one. Practice makes you better. Finally I did not care how many people I talked too. Our Diamond Don Altman started coming to Rome. We would meet at Shoney's Restaurant on Turner McCall Boulevard. They had a meeting room and we would invite people to go with us. Don did a very good job of showing the plan. I started to read lots of good books, *Think and Grow Rich*, *How to Win Friends and Influence People*, *The Magic of Thinking Big*, and so on. Don's organization was slowly growing and it was like one big family. Every so often, Don would have a big rally in this area. He would invite good speakers and we would leave the rally very excited and motivated. We were moving on up. Things changed, Don teams up with another diamond, Tom Crisp. Tom is a fireball speaker and I thought we were going places now. Under Don's organization you could buy tapes and books when you wanted to. Now they started tape of the week and book of the month and you had to take them. You had no choice. The rallies were now far off like Dallas Tulsa, and Chicago. We were now selling tapes, books, and rallies, not Amway. I rent a motor home for some of my people to drive to Chicago. Mary and I fly to Chicago for the big rally. It cost lots of money for people to attend these rallies. At first there were big crowds at these rallies. The crowd was not as big at Chicago. After the rally was over, our direct said, "We got tickets for your people to buy for the next rally. You owe us money for these tickets and it's got to be paid now."

I looked at Kathy and said, "There is no way I will do that."

She said, "You have got to."

And I said, "Sorry, it won't happen."

I then walked off. I figured not enough people came to help cover the cost of holding the rally. Mary and I went to the airport to catch the plane home. I was standing in the airport looking at a severe thunderstorm coming at us. I was thinking if that storm hits while the plane is on the ground I will not get on that plane. We finally took off and flew into that storm. The lightning was so bad it seemed like someone was turning a light switch on and off. It was a rough ride going through that thunderstorm and I was nervous. After that rally, the business went downhill. They had drained the people. Within a year, I was out of the business. Amway is a good company and it was not their fault. I learned a lot and it turned my life around. Like good food turned my life around. I got involved in running Brannon Bros. Roofing Co. And I moved on.

In the late eighties, I always had an upset stomach and had to watch what I ate. I went to see Doctor Keith Parmer, and he said, "I am going to have you admitted to Redmond Park Hospital and run some tests." A few days later, I was admitted to Redmond Park Hospital. That afternoon, the doctor came into my room and said, "In the morning, Redmond is going to have you drink a white liquid, do not drink or eat anything tonight. They will do a CAT SCAN on you."

The next morning they came and got me. Lisa Broadway, a good friend, was one of the nurses taking care of me. I drank this white liquid, and then they put me in the CAT SCAN. It was hot in there and Lisa came over and said, "We have got to rearrange you."

I said, "Good, I am burning up in here."

She said, "It is not supposed to be hot in there, you are turning red." She said to an assistant, "Get the doctor, he must be allergic to what he drank."

The doctor came in and said, "Get the Benadryl in him fast, hurry, get it in him." My eyes and lips had swollen shut. He said, "Are you having problems breathing?"

I said, "No, but I am fixing to pass out."

He said, "Get more Benadryl in him."

A few minutes later I started getting better and having Lisa there helped keep me calm. Three days later my skin was still a light red and I looked like boiled shrimp. I still had an upset stomach.

In 1990, Mount Berry Square Mall was being built on US 27 north of Rome in the Armuchee area. We got the contract to roof 75 percent of this new mall. You could stand at one end of the mall on the roof and you could not recognize the person on the other end of the mall. The contractor building the new mall gave us a very hard time because we had to have access to the roof. The contractor would not let us stack our material close to the new mall being built. We had to haul the material the long way on a forklift and then lift it up to the roof. The developer had an inspector to stay with us to make sure that the new roof was put on correctly. After a few weeks, he said, "You guys know what you are doing and y'all do not need me up here anymore." The inspector was on our side and he would give us some good advice on how to handle the general contractor. We had a time limit to get this roofing job done and if we could not meet this time limit we would be fined seven hundred dollars a day until the job was completed. We went to work every day at 6:00 a.m. and quit at 6:00 p.m. seven days a week.

We were lucky because it was early spring that we were roofing the mall and best I remember it only rained about three or four times and that was at night. We were roofing the mall in early part of the spring and it was not too hot or not too cold. Thank goodness we had good weather. I lost two inches in my waist from walking so much while installing the new roof.

Yes, we made our deadline and had one week to spare. It was a close call. We were now the largest roofing company in northwest Georgia.

In 1990, my sister Barbara and her husband, Dayton Miller, came to Rome to visit with us. They moved to Tucson, Arizona, in 1968. It had been twenty-two years since I had seen them. Dayton showed his age but Barbara looked about the same as when she left. I thought she really had taken good care of herself. She went around with a cigarette and a cup of coffee in her hand all the time. They stayed for a week and we really enjoyed having them. They left and went back to Arizona. About a year later, I had just got to the office getting ready for work. Glenn walked into the office, called me and Grady together, and said, "I got bad news. Dayton called and he said Barbara died from lung cancer. She will be buried today. Barbara would not let him tell anyone, she did not want to worry us." We all decided to go to work because there was nothing we could do about it now. I wanted to go to work and I shed a lot of tears. Work helped to keep my mind busy.

My son Joel and I were riding through Lindale when a horse with this young lady riding it came toward us. The horse was running as hard as it could go. The horse was running down Park Avenue in Lindale when it came across the bridge in front of the mill. The young lady had the horse's head pulled completely sideways trying to stop him. The horse hit a power pole and it knocked her off and she went flying through the air and hit the pavement very hard. I stopped and if I would have had a cell phone I would have called 911 the first thing then checked on her. About that time a young man came riding up on a horse and we checked on her. I said, "I think we need to call an ambulance." He said, "Can you help me set her on the back tail gate of your truck and take her down the street and go down to the creek where her parents are?" I carried her down to her parents and left her with them. Later I found out she had broken her leg.

Another time I was traveling down Cedar Avenue in East Rome and a pretty young lady was riding her horse pretty fast right inside her fenced-in pasture. All of a sudden the horse stepped in a ditch and fell forward right on top of the young lady. The young lady was lying there gasping for her breath and I thought she was dying. I had a phone in my truck that I had to leave in the truck to use. I called 911 and said, "Send an ambulance, a horse has just fell on top of a young girl." I told her my location. About that time, the young lady jumped up and I said, "Don't move I have an ambulance on the way." She said, "I am okay," and walked off. She must have had the breath knocked out of her and it sure did scare me. Until this day I do not ride horses and I am scared of them.

On March 13, 1993, Rome and Floyd County had a blizzard and I mean a bad one. It was Friday night and I was having a few drinks at the Landings Restaurant with friends when I noticed it had started snowing. The weather forecast was for a few inches of snow later that night. I had already had a bad experience of being caught on the road and almost not getting home because of snow. A few years earlier I was at home and it started snowing and we had a maid cleaning the house. We lived in Wax and she lived about twelve miles away close to downtown Rome. I said, "I need to take you home before it gets too bad." I left around 3:00 p.m. and by the time I got her home sleet began to mix with the snow. It took me several hours to get out of downtown Rome and I decided not to try and go the Rockmart Highway because it was a road of nothing but hills. I decided to go through Lindale because there were no hills through Lindale to get home. It was very slow driving and traffic was bumper to bumper and very slow. I turned left on the Old Rockmart Road and I had about two miles to go before I would get to the Wax Road where I would turn left and go home. Just before I got to Wax Road, there was a long, small hill to go up. Now it was getting dark and when I got there cars were backed up and in the ditches and the road was impassable. Now what am I going to do? I decided to try one more route and I went back, turned left on Reesburg Road, went a few miles and turned left on Donahue Road. I knew there was a small short hill that would be my only obstacle to get home. I started up the hill and only made it about halfway so I backed up and tried again and made it a little farther. I thought, I've got to get over that hill or I have got about five miles to walk home and I was not dressed for it. I backed up as far as I could and I really gave my truck lots of gas and it was slipping and sliding and it was hard to hold it in the road. This was my third try and I just did make it to the top of the hill and boy what a relief that was. There were no hills to speak of going home now coming back there was one but I was going home and it was downhill and I got home around 9:00 p.m. and I was one happy person.

I now lived in North Lindale and it was time to go home. I left the restaurant and by the time I got home it was snowing very hard so I left my truck parked at the convenience store at the bottom of the hill. I lived about two blocks up a steep hill and I would at least have a way to get around the next day. I walked up the hill to my house. Our house was total electric and in a few hours the power went off. The wind was blowing very hard and the snow was very heavy and you could not see very far. I remember seeing a movie of a frontier man lost in a blizzard. He was lost and could not find his way home. The next day after the storm had stopped they found him dead about a hundred feet from his cabin. I remember thinking how he could not find his cabin that close to it. Now I understand when you can only see a couple of feet in front of you. I had seen my first blizzard. Tree limbs were breaking because of the heavy snow and wind blowing and it sounded like cannons going off. Also I could hear explosions going off and I thought transformers were blowing up then it hit me those weren't the transformers blowing up because there was no power. I started looking outside and I saw blue lighting and it was the thunder making the noise. The next day we still had phone service and I called a friend of mine who managed the Ramada Inn in Rome on Turner McCall Blvd. and I told her my situation and she said, "If you can get here I have a place for you to stay." The only people who had power was the downtown area. We packed our clothes and first Joel and I walked down to see if I would be able to drive my truck. We waded in the snow which was about two feet deep and when we got to my truck the snow was so deep I could not move it. I stood there thinking what I was going to do. We had no power and no heat. About that time Phillip Broadaway, who I had rented my basement to, came driving by in his four wheel drive truck. I flagged him down and I told him our situation and could he take us to Ramada Inn and he said sure. Thank goodness his four wheel truck set up high. We all walked up the hill got Mary and went to Ramada Inn. It was a rough life no TV to watch but we had lights and I would have to sit at the bar at night drinking my crown and seven.

Ronnie Corntassel, a friend of mine who worked for Georgia Power Co., was stranded in the mountain area of the northwest section of Floyd County. He radioed for help and it took hours for Georgia Power to rescue him. They had to cut trees out of the roads and use their heavy duty four-wheel-drive trucks to get to him. Two couples went out joy riding in the storm and got stranded on one of the mountains north of Floyd County. The two men decided to walk for help. They did not make it and were found dead the next day. Like I said, it was a bad blizzard.

Larry Lemming, a friend of mine, lived on the Reesburg Road about eight miles south of downtown Rome and Floyd Hospital. Larry got into a fuss fight with his wife and he was lying on the couch when she walked in and started shooting him and he jumped up, ran out of the house, and ran about two hundred feet and he collapsed and fell into the deep snow. He had been shot several times. Friends called 911 but it took hours to get to him due to the blizzard. It took a long time to get him to Floyd Hospital and if it had not been for all that snow around him he would have died.

Thank goodness the weather warmed up in a few days and the roads were opened up and Georgia Power was able to get the power back on. We had lots of work to do because of the trees that had fallen on the roofs as well as wind damage to roofs. A few days later, Ashley Bender called and said, "I have roof leaks, can you come and check my roof?" I went by to check on her roof and she took me up in the attic and showed me the leaks. I went up on the roof and checked out the situation and said I could send someone over to fix the roof. Ashley said, "How much will it cost?" I said, "About $150." She put her hands on me and said, "Thank you." The chemistry between us was unreal so we grabbed each other and I kissed her and she said, "I got to sit down I think I am going to pass out." After that I said, "I got to go." She asked, "How can I see you again?" and I said, "Call me and say you got another roof leak." I kissed her and left and started driving down the road and it hit me what the hell was I doing. I had never done anything like that before. I thought I will probably be arrested or killed by a jealous husband tomorrow. I almost hyperventilated and thought I was dying. A few days later she called me and said her husband was in the hospital with a light heart attack but it was not serious and she would call me as soon as she could.

A few weeks went by and I thought that was the end of that situation. A few days later she called and said her husband Dan had gone back to work and she had a roof leak and to come over to check her roof. We talked and made plans to see each other in a few days. I had one problem, what was I going to do with a red truck with advertisement on it? I have a good friend, Bradley Roberson, who runs a used car lot on Shorter Avenue in West Rome. I stopped by for a visit and I told him my problem. Bradley said, "Just leave your truck here and I will loan you a car." I said, "Good idea" and he gave me keys to one of his cars. I got the car and started driving down Shorter Avenue heading toward East Rome. Willey, who takes care of his cars and works on them, came into his office and said, "Where is he going in that car?" and Bradley said, "Over to East Rome," and he said, "He will never make it. The front end is about to fall out from under it." After I had driven several blocks the car starts shaking real bad. I slowed down and just a few blocks from my destination, it gets to shaking and rattling so bad I had to stop, get out, and look around and under the car but I could not see anything wrong. I got back in and drove very slow until I got there. After several hours of visiting with Ashley I headed back to West Rome and I drove very, very slowly and several times I almost got rear-ended. When I pulled into his lot, I told him, "What the hell, were you trying to kill me?"

Bradley said he did not know anything was wrong with it until Willey came in and told him. He said he would make it up to me and next time give me a nice car.

On April 4, 1994, I was watching the weather on Channel 2 and they were predicting severe storms for that afternoon. I noticed the dew point was in low 70s. I thought it looked like we were going to have some severe weather that day. I walked outside to get the newspaper. I looked up at the clouds and they were moving very fast. I looked around and there was nothing moving on the ground. It was so still and it was scary. I thought I had better go over to our office and warehouse and prepare for storms. Our business was located at Six Miles at the intersection of US 27 and US 411. This area in Floyd County is known as tornado alley. I read the paper and ate breakfast and then headed over to our business. I was in the office when Jeff Brannon, my nephew who worked for us, came in. I said, "Jeff, I want you to go turn our trucks around facing east." Jeff asked why, and I said, "Trust me, you are going to see the worst storm you have ever seen today." He looked at me with a serious look and he went and moved the trucks. Our big trucks have a steel bed with a steel cab cover on them. The tornados will come out of the west and I thought this would at least keep the windshields from being broken. At about 1:00 p.m., I heard that a tornado hit a church in Piedmont, Alabama, and killed lots of people. Piedmont is about forty miles west of Rome. Later I heard trees were down on Second Avenue in East Rome. I drove to Rome to see what had happened. There were several large trees blown down on East Second Ave. The tornado hit Mt. Alto which was the southwest section of Rome and the mountain busted up the tornado. After that Jeff said, "I thought you were crazy but now if you say it's going to rain I will believe you."

Sam and his family were at Cheryl's mom's house on the Old Cedartown Highway when Sam heard that a tornado was headed toward Lindale. Sam said, "Okay, let's go to the storm shelter." Sam and the kids hurried to get in the storm shelter. Cheryl and her mom Phyllis Groves just took their time. Sam hollered, "Cheryl, hurry, it is coming."

Cheryl said, "You get too excited."

About that time the tornado hit about a quarter mile south of them. A piece of plywood and leaves went sailing up around them. They started screaming and running as fast as they could.

My nephew, Donnie Canada, was visiting with me in North Lindale. Donnie was a City of Rome policeman and he had his police radio with him. We would listen to the police radio and watch all of the emergency vehicles going by in front of my house. I had two nice rental houses in the Conn Lakes subdivision. The next day I rode down to see about them. The police had roads blocked off. I pulled up to the road block and I was in my work truck. The police asked me why I needed to go in. I said, "I have two houses and I need to check on them." They motioned me on through. I drove into the subdivision to check to see how much damage was done to my houses. I was very surprised. At the first house, only one wall was standing at the bathroom with a large timber sticking through it. At the second house, no walls were standing. The first house there was a couple in it. They got in a closet and when the storm was over the floor had opened up and they fell to the ground under the house. The second house the young couple and their kids laid down in the hall. The hall wall fell on them and saved their lives. The tornado destroyed 75 percent of that subdivision.

The First Baptist Church in Lindale was having a special Easter Sunday service. Majority of the people who lived in that subdivision were at church. That church service saved lots of lives. Across the road and up on top of a hill a young girl was visiting with friends. They were sitting in the carport talking when the owner looked out and saw it coming. He said, "Run, let's get in this ditch." They did and a large tree fell on the young girl. She was paralyzed from the waist down. That was the only serious injury. Several days later they were roofing a house and Jeff called and said, "Do we need to keep tearing off the old shingles? It sure does look like rain."

I had just seen the weather at the office and the dew point was in the low 40s. I said, "Yes, keep tearing, it is not going to rain."

He said, "You sure? It is very cloudy and sure looks like rain."

I said, "Tear it off."

Jeff said, "Okay, that is what we will do."

I went back later that afternoon and parked my truck and got in the Buick and headed down Shorter Avenue feeling like a big Indian. I looked down at the gas hand and it's on empty so I pulled into a convenience store to get gas. I pulled up beside a gas pump to get gas and walked back to take off the gas cap but I needed keys to unlock it. I turned around get the keys and guess what, they don't work. What am I going to do? Then I decided to go down to our warehouse and knock the cap off. It was about six miles away and now I look back, what a stupid idea that was. I got down there and started to try and knock it off when I realized I was stupid. "You are going to blow yourself up." I fixed myself a crown and seven and I was mad as hell and headed back to West Rome to take that dam car back. While I was driving back, I got to thinking, here I am drinking, what am I going to do if I run out of gas and I thought if I run out I am going to jump out and run like hell. Well, I made it back and got my truck and drove back to East Rome and parked at a garage about four blocks away. I got my crown bottle and two 7-Ups, put them in a shack and crossed Turner McCall Boulevard, a very busy highway. I was lucky I was not run over. Finally I got there and Ashley was going to leave the upstairs back door unlocked for me. What a relief it was. I had finally made it, or had I? I got to the top of the stairs and stopped on the landing reached for the door knob and it would not open and about that time a car was pulling into the back parking area and stopped. I thought what am I going to do it is too late to leave and where would I go so I just leaned against the door and froze and expecting any minute for that lady that got out of her car to start screaming. Lucky for me, she never looked up and went in downstairs and in just a few seconds later Ashley opened the door. Ashley said her son Scott happened to walk by the door, saw it was unlocked, and he locked it.

Next day I carried the keys back and I told Bradley what happened and he thought it was very funny but I did not and yes he sold the car that day. I could see Ashley in the day time because her husband worked in Atlanta and he was at home at night and the weekends but after about one and a half years later he was transferred to Oklahoma City, Oklahoma. Ashley had to stay in Rome to run the business and I had lots of rental property and we would make one of them our love shack.

I had a love shack in North Rome and Charles Griffin, a friend of mine, loaned me his old Cimarron Cadillac to drive. I would park it in the garage, leave the keys in it, and locked the garage door. When I wanted to go see Ashley, I would park my truck behind the house and drive the car. Ashley's son Scott and his two children needed a place to temporarily live, so I let them move in. Ashley called me and said Scott had stolen the car, come pick her up, I know about the area where he might be at. I go by pick her up and we drive around in the East Rome area looking for the car and we had just about to give up when she said, "Let's go down this dead end street," our last place to look. We drove down the street, did not see anything, and turned around started back when I spotted the car parked behind this house. We were in a bad neighborhood and I stopped, got out, knocked on the door, and a man came to the door. I asked, "Is Scott here?" and he said, "He just ran out the back door." I told him, "He stole that car and I need to get it back." The man said Scott pawned it to him for three hundred dollars and he had a signed receipt and when he gets his money back I can have the car. I said, "That car is stolen and I need to get it back or I will have to call the police." He said, "No money, no car." I turned, walked back to the car and told Ashley what he said. She said, "Don't you owe him some money for working on your rental property? How much do you have?" I counted my money and I had $180. I go back to the house and said, "Look, we have two choices. I have $180 for you or I will call the police." He looked at me and said, "Okay." I gave him the money and he gave me the keys and I went got the car and we got out of there as fast as we could.

Later I rented one of my houses in the Coosa area to Ashley's daughter in-law, Scott's ex-wife. Carrie and Ashley's two grandkids and her boyfriend lived there for about six months. They moved out and we made that house our new love shack.

About two months later I got a call from the lady I knew and a friend of ours. She called and said, "You need to come we need to talk now."

I said, "I am very sick I will come later."

She said, "You need to come now it's very important."

She only lived about a mile from me so I get up to leave and Mary said, "Where are you going? You are sick."

I said, "I am going to collect the rent money I will be okay."

I get there and she said, "I got some bad news. Mary knows where your love shack is in Coosa."

I said, "How she found out?"

She said, "A Georgia power bill came to where you live and she started snooping." The lady said she did not know for sure but she was going to start snooping around very soon. I left and called Ashley and I said, "I have bad news, Mary has found out about our love shack, take your truck now and go get the TV and our personal things out."

She said, "I will leave now."

A few days later Mary went down there to the neighbors' houses asking questions and they told her a couple with a red Ford truck had lived there. I drove a red Dodge truck.

After Ashley's husband, Dan moved to Oklahoma, I made friends with her mom and dad and her mom would tell Ashley, "Why don't you marry Roy?" I was one of the family and spent lots of time there. The insurance company her husband worked for decided to downsize and he went around to the insurance branches that were not making money and shut them down. He would take a policeman with him, walk into their office, and announce, "We are closing this office down and you have fifteen minutes to get your personal things out." That went on for about a year and one day the top executive's walked into his office and gave him the same news.

All good things come to an end. Ashley's husband came home and they sold the apartment building and moved to

Gulf Shores, Alabama. I made a few trips down to see her but is very hard to do. They divorced and she had met another roofer, Bruce Johnston. He also drove a red truck and they got married.

End of Brannon Brothers

After forty years of a very successful roofing business, Glenn and Grady decided to retire. In 1998 we began to close the roofing business down. I decided to go on in the roofing business with Johnny Rogers. Johnny was our commercial estimator and he was very good at it. Late in 1998, our secretary, Resa Toles, walked into my office and said, "I want you to call this psychic, Kelly Joe."

I said, "Resa, I don't believe in that stuff."

Resa said her friends had called Kelly Joe and things had come true for them. "Please call her for me."

"Okay, you call her and I will talk to her."

she called Kelly Joe. I did this for Resa and she dialed the number and gave me the phone. Resa said, "Tell her to do a reading on you." Kelly Jo answered the phone and I said, "I want You to do a reading." Kelly Jo said a little prayer and she said, "I see you are going into business for yourself." Well, I thought does she knows that. Kelly Jo then said, "I see your wife is going to be very helpful to you in your new business."

I said, "You don't know what the hell you are talking about."

I started to hang up and Kelly Jo said, "Oh, yes. I don't normally talk negative but this time I will. Your present wife who is short, plump, and dark hair and very, very depressed."

My heart almost stopped she described Mary to a tee. She said, "If you don't divorce her you will die from stomach problems. You are having stomach problems right now." I said yes. She said, "You will divorce her and take good care of her. You are a man of your word. You will meet a lady about forty-nine years old and very slim and her hair was reddish blonde." Kelly Jo said, "A man with white hair would come to you with a business deal, trust him."

Well, next three months, nothing happened. We auctioned off Brannon Brothers' roofing property on March 24, 1999, and my share was very good. You could only call Kelly Joe ever three months and in the early 1999 I called her. Kelly Joe told me about the same thing except Kelly Jo said, "You will meet a lady and her hair is the color of a small blond kid sitting in the evening sunset and she had two kids one at home and one lived away."

I went to lunch with Johnny Rogers at Applebee's and Bobby Priest Wheeler was our server. She said she had just moved to Lindale and needed a plumber. I gave her the number of my plumber. I told her I owned lots a rental property and he took care of my plumbing problems. A few weeks later, Johnny, Resa, and I went to have lunch at Applebee's and Bobbie was again our server. We did not flirt with each other, just business as usual, and a few weeks later we auctioned off Brannon Brothers' property. One morning I was going down the Rockmart Highway and passed a friend of mine who was coming out of a side road and he started blowing his horn and waving at me and I thought he was just being friendly to me. It was Charles Griffin, a real estate agent, and he followed me and got me to pull over.

Charles said, "I know how you can keep from paying taxes on that money." I asked how, and he said, "I could do a 1031 exchange."

I said, "What is a 1031?"

He told me, "When you sell property and buy new property you pay no taxes."

I said, "Let me talk to my accountant." I called my accountant, Skip House, and set up a meeting that day. Skip said, "Yes, I could do that." I told Charles, "I wanted to buy a condo in Gulf Shores, Alabama." Charles said okay and we planned a trip to Alabama. Charles had a friend, Myra Greene, who owned a condo there. Myra put Charles in touch with Keith Morris, and we were going down to meet him on a Friday. Charles has white hair. Tuesday, May 7, 1999, I was driving down Turner McCall Boulevard and to this day I do not know what made me all of a sudden turn to go to Applebee's. I had made no plans to go and talk to Bobbie.

I went into the restaurant and said, "I want Bobbie's table." The hostess took me over to her table. Bobbie came over to my table and I said, "I am a married man but very unhappy and I want to take you out to dinner, but not this Friday but next Friday in Cartersville, Georgia." Cartersville was a town about twenty-five miles east of Rome.

Bobbie answered, "Why not Atlanta?"

"Okay," I said, "it's a date."

I could not go that Friday because Charles and I were going to Gulf Shores, Alabama, to buy a condo. Bobbie's hair was lite reddish blonde and she had two daughters Crystal who lived in Colorado Springs, Colorado, and Shannon who lived with Bobbie in Lindale. May 1999 I went to Gulf Shores. Charles and I rented a condo and the next morning we were going to meet with Keith. Charles has MS and walks with a limp. We get up the next morning and get ready and I notice Charles drinks 2 Diet Pepsi while we were getting ready. We go to a restaurant to eat breakfast and we sit down. I ordered coffee and Charles ordered coffee and a Diet Pepsi and we go to the buffet and fix our breakfast. We sit down and start eating and Charles said, to the server, "Can I have another Diet Pepsi?"

I look at Charles and I said, "How many of those things do you drink a day?"

He said, "Oh, about twenty a day."

I said, "You wonder what's wrong with you, read the contents they have aspartame in red letters and that means bad news. Red means danger and I understand from what I have read aspartame could cause MS."

We met up with Keith and he took us around and showed us some condos to buy. We went to look at a new condo that was being built in Orange Beach, Alabama, which is right next to Gulf Shores, Alabama. I bought a two-bedroom, two-bath corner penthouse unit on the top floor and a one-bedroom unit next door. The name of the condo was Tradewinds.

Instead of dinner in Atlanta, I met Bobbie at my love shack in West Rome. I cooked steak (which I burned). Shannon dropped Bobbie off and it was our first date even though Bobbie did not enjoy that burnt steak. We hit it off and Bobbie and I knew we were meant for each other.

My New Life

Mary and I had drifted apart and in 1999, I divorced Mary. Like Kelly Jo said, I would take very good care of her. In 2001, Bobbie and I flew to Las Vegas to get married. We had already made arrangements with Little Chapel of Flowers. We stayed at the Luxor Casino, a pyramid shaped casino in Las Vegas. The Little Chapel of Flowers sent a big limo over to pick us up. We had to pay the driver thirty-five dollars and the limo took us on Sunday to a wedding shop and we rented the clothes we needed. After that the limo carried us to the courthouse to get our marriage license. On the way back, Bobbie said to the driver, "I wish Elvis could give me away." The driver handed Bobbie a card of an Elvis impersonator, saying he was very good.

On May 7, 2001, (our first date was May 7, 1999) we were to be married at 5:30 that afternoon. That morning I got up and went down to the casino and started playing slot machines. I was playing the slots when I hit $500.00 and I moved over to the next slot machine while waiting for the casino host to come and pay me. I had put a $100.00 in the other slot machine beside me. I had built it up to $350.00 when Bobbie came up. I got up from that slot machine and told Bobbie to play it and when it comes back down to three hundred she should cash out. Bobbie cashed out and went to the pool and had several drinks and bought a nice set of sunglasses. Bobbie then went and had her hair fixed and it looked gorgeous. She went back up to the room and called the Elvis impersonator. She had $125.00 left and Elvis wanted $300 but Bobbie told him, "I have only $125 and have no family or friends here to attend my wedding." Elvis asked what time our wedding was. Bobbie told him, and Elvis said, "Well, I'm already going to be there at 5:00 p.m." Elvis was going to renew an older couple's wedding vows. Bobbie said she would pay him cash. The Elvis impersonator said he would do it.

Our room was in the back of the Luxor Casino. We had to walk through the front of the casino to catch our limo. People were clapping and wishing us good luck. When we got to the Little Flowers Wedding Chapel and our time came, we went in the room and the preacher went over what to do. Bobbie left us and went out front and they started playing the music. Bobbie was very excited that Elvis was escorting her down the aisle. Bobbie's family in Athens, Alabama, and my son, Sam and his family in Lindale, Georgia, were watching it live on the Internet. Elvis sang several songs to us and I was thinking, *Bobbie's going to say I want Elvis, not you Roy.* I would not have been surprised if she had said that. After the preacher married us we three finished singing "Viva Las Vegas." It was a very exciting wedding.

Bobbie called home to see if her parents had seen it. Bobbie's mother, Betty Ann, said yes. Will Priest, Bobbie's nephew who was fourteen at the time, said, "Nanny, who did she marry, Elvis or Roy?" After the wedding the limo took us back to the Luxor. We had to walk all the way through the casino and people congratulated us again. That was a very special day.

Back to the Real World

After Brannon Brothers closed down, I started Roy B Brannon Roof Masters Incorporated. I took care of residential roofing and my partner, Johnny Rogers, took care of commercial roofing. Resa Toles was our secretary who ran the office. In December 2002, things did not work out as I had planned. Two of our trucks had wrecks and due to the heat that summer we made very little profit. Our insurance went up and up so I decided to close down and do residential roofing out of my house. Bobbie could tear off and clean up as good as anybody. Me and a couple more guys would go out and do residential roofing.

I will never forget we went down to Lake Weiss to roof a cabin which was just across the Alabama line. We did not finish this roof and had to come back the next day. We had to throw some scrap roofing over on the backside of the roof in a valley. I told Bobbie, "Go over on the backside and clean the waste roofing out of the valley." Bobbie started cleaning the old roofing up and all of a sudden started screaming, "Snake, snake in this trash!" She started running back over to the front of the roof. Alonzo and I jumped up and ran across the roof to see what was going on and there was a small rattlesnake in the valley. But it ran off the roof and Alonzo went down and killed it. Bobbie was very mad and wanted to know why I did not tell her there were snakes on the roof. I told Bobbie that was the first time I had ever seen a snake on a roof. Bobbie would not clean the ground up after that.

I could tell you when it was going to rain. My arthritis would flare up on me and I could hardly work. I would have to take a couple of Aleve pills and about thirty minutes later I would be able to work but very slow. We were working in West Rome roofing a house when all of a sudden my arthritis really flared up on me very bad. I said, "Okay, guys, rain is very close." They said to me there's no rain in the forecast for that day. I told them it was coming, and I went and laid down in my truck. I was not able to work. I told them they had about two hours to finish the roof. Approximately two hours later, it started to rain just as they were finishing up.

Bobbie and I bought a two-bedroom, one–bath, small wood frame house in West Rome just off Martha Berry Boulevard. We would invite our four grandchildren over to spend the weekends with us. Their ages were from three to six years old. Luke was the oldest then Taylor and Tucker and Bonnie was the youngest. These grandchildren had the run of the house and if our kids had done half of what they did there was no telling what we would have done to them. This house was very small and we just did not have enough room so we decided to sell and we did. We bought a three-bedroom two-bath house in Twikenham Estates on the east side of Rome. Shannon brought home a little blonde puppy that she had rescued because its mother had died after giving birth and Shannon could hold it in the palm of her hand. Shannon fed this little puppy with an eye dropper and named her Sadie. Sadie was half poodle and half Chihuahua and had a champagne color. Shannon had to move and where she was moving did not allow pets so Shannon brought Sadie to stay with us. I was raised that dogs were not allowed in the house. We gave Sadie to the little girl who lived next door to us and Bobbie said if it does not work out she would take Sadie back. Well, it did not work out and Bobbie got Sadie back. I did not like it but I had to give in and take Sadie back. Sadie learned real fast and it was not long after she was house broken. Sadie had short curly hair and she did not shed. You could wear dark pants and let her sit in your lap and you would never know that a dog had been in your lap. Sadie became one of the family, and she would know what you were talking about. Bobbie's sister, Debbie Gable, was sitting on the couch and holding Sadie. Debbie said, "Bobbie, I think this dog needs a bath." Sadie turns on Debbie and tries to eat her up and she pushed her out of her lap. Debbie looks at Bobbie and said, "What's wrong with this damn crazy dog?" I said, "Debbie, don't say bath." In the daytime, Sadie sits in my lap and if Bobbie comes up close to me she will try to eat her up. Sadie has to be right next to Bobbie when we go to sleep. When Bobbie gets up, Sadie gets up. I thought I was tied down with kids, try going somewhere with your pet. It is very hard to find a place that allows pets. It was a lot easier to leave kids with somebody than a pet. When we did find someone, Sadie would hardly eat until we got back. That was the reason we became pet friendly with our condos.

Bobbie's mom went into the hospital to have an operation. Bobbie told her mom we did not have anywhere to leave Sadie and that I would have to stay home to take care of her. Betty Ann had been to our house and she loved Sadie but Bill did not allow anyone to bring a dog in his house. Mom said, "Bring Sadie with you, it will be okay." She was a smoker and due to her smoking she was going to have a straw inserted in an artery in her leg. We drove up to be with her and we carried Sadie because we had nowhere to leave her. When we got to their house, Bobbie went over to visit with her mom and I stayed behind with Sadie. I had Sadie on a leash. I was sitting there with Sadie on a leash in their living room and Bill said, "I have washed a coon cage out so we can put the dog in it and leave it outside for the night." I was very nervous because we were not going to leave her outside. Bobbie would go crazy when she heard about this. Bill said, "Turn that dog loose." I said, "Bill, she will jump up in your lap," and he said again, "Turn her loose." I turned her loose and sure enough she runs and jumps in his lap and Bill pets her. Bill took a liking to her. Lately, if we were going up for a visit, Bill wants to make sure we bring Sadie with us.

Moving to Alabama

I n 2003, we auctioned off all of our rental property in Rome and we bought a two-bedroom, two-bath unit at Crystal Shores in Gulf Shores, Alabama. This was a condo under construction and we now had three condos and Four Seasons Rental Management ran these properties for us and did a very good job.

In 2004, Hurricane Ivan hit Pensacola, Florida and Orange Beach, Alabama, which was next to the Florida line and Gulf Shores, Alabama. Tradewinds was heavily damaged and the pool was completely gone. The first floor was taken out. The units on the back side from the first through the thirteenth floors had all the doors, furniture, and windows blown out. If you had been in one of those units, you would not have survived the storm. There was a car upside down in front of our condo out in the ocean about seventy-five feet from the shoreline. It was upside down with the wheels sticking out of the water. Where that car came from I did not know. We heard that the ocean came up eight foot high and a twenty-three-foot wave on top of that as well as the hurricane winds. It took a long time to get Tradewinds back up before we could start renting the units. Crystal Shores did not get that much damage, thank goodness. We were very fortunate to have insurance that covered our rental losses on our units. Today you cannot get that kind of insurance coverage and there are only two insurance companies that will write insurance and it is expensive on the buildings. At Crystal Shores, the sand was so high you had to duck your head to walk on the parking area directly under the condo.

Bobbie, Shannon Wheeler, my stepdaughter, and I came down to Gulf Shores to check on our condos. They would not let us through to check on them because roads were washed out and lots of sand and debris was in the roads. The Alabama National Guard was guarding the roads going in. All trucks were stopped and inspected coming out of Gulf Shore and I wondered what in the world they were looking for. Well, I found out you would be in deep trouble if they caught you sneaking sand out. We could not find anywhere to stay, so I called the casinos in Mississippi. I got us a room at the Grand Casino in Gulfport, Mississippi. We drove over to Gulfport and checked in at the Grand Casino. I had six free nights and I had to pay only $49 for one night. Free nights, yes. We gambled a lot at Grand Casino and in other places. We carried $1,300 dollars with us and we gambled every night with caution. We had to check out Sunday and Saturday night was our last night to stay. Our money was running low and I started watching this lady playing a dollar machine and she was putting lots of money into it. Finally she got up and I went over, sat down, and started playing. After a few plays, I hit $300. Bobbie and Shannon came by and said they were going upstairs to the bathroom. There were machines against the wall right behind were I had just won the $300. A lady got up from one of them so I go and sit down. I had never seen these machines, they were red eights and I started playing and after a few plays I hit $300. I moved over to the next one and again $300. Next one, $300. The lady who had got up from the first machine said, "Hey, lucky, you want this machine"? I said, "Why not?" I got up, went over, and after a few plays I hit $350. I had four machines lit up on that wall and I collected my tickets and I went upstairs to cash in my tickets. I had been playing other machines and my total tickets were $1,698. They paid me and about that time Bobbie and Shannon came out of the bathroom. I held up the money and said, "While yawl was in the bathroom, look what I have won."

Bobbie said, "Give me half."

I said, "No, we going home with extra money."

She said, "That's part of my money."

I said no again and again. but when she kept insisting I gave her $98. I could not believe she settled for it. We went down the escalator and to the $1 machines. Bobbie sat down at one and started playing and she looked at me and asked me to play on the one next to her I said I wasn't going to spend any of this money. Bobbie sticks a $20 bill in my machine and, yes, after a few plays I hit $200. Bobbie had moved to a table behind me and she hit $300. We get and go over to the escalator that led to the bridge over to the hotel. We are going by the last machines just before you cross over to the hotel and Bobbie said, "Let me play these machines." I said, "Bobbie, it's 3:00 a.m. and way past our bedtime." She was insistent, so I told her okay. She sat down at a twenty-five-cent machine and started playing. Again she asked me to play and I said no, so she stuck a $20 bill in my machine. Yes, after a few plays, I hit $300. I got up and cashed in and as was I walking back when the couple playing next to us said, "Hey, I hear you are mister lucky." I said, "Yes, let me touch you on your head." She said, "No, play my machine one time." I reached down, touched the play button, and she hit big time. She hit like triple, triple, and double diamonds but she was only playing five cents so she won $70. I said, "From now on, you play only quarters." She did and later she hit $200. After I got back a few minutes later, Bobbie hit $300 and we go to bed. We turned that $98 dollars into $1,100 and we were two happy people. It was our lucky day.

Our Gambling Trips

Another time Bobbie and I flew out of Atlanta, I don't remember the name of the airline, but the flight was mainly for people going to Reno, Nevada, to gamble. We were flying to Reno when the pilot came on the intercom and said, "Ladies and gentlemen, they are having a snowstorm in Reno and we'll have to detour to Sacramento, California."

We landed in Sacramento and the captain came on the intercom and said, "Ladies and gentlemen, we do not have landing rights for this airport and you will have to stay on the plane and we will go ahead and refuel." After about two hours, the captain said, "Ladies and gentlemen, we have been cleared for takeoff."

Going over the Sierra Mountains to Sacramento, the trip was a little bumpy. On our return trip back over the Sierra Mountains to go to Reno, when we crossed those mountains, we hit some down draft from air going down the side of the mountain. The plane started dropping two hundred to three hundred feet it seemed like and people started screaming and hollering. At one time the plane turned up almost sideways and then I was scared. At first I was not scared. Brad Miller, a friend of mine who I was in the Amway business, told me about him flying over Stone Mountain, in Georgia. He said, "I had put the flaps down on the plane to slow down and enjoy the view. After I had crossed the mountain, the plane went into a nose dive, and I could not pull out of it. I finally realized I had put the flaps down and I pulled out just in time." He said, "After I passed over the mountain, the wind started pulling me down, and it was a very close call. Finally the plane leveled out."

When we got into Reno I knew why we did not try to land in Reno. You would have had to fly in between mountains and I mean mountains, and we landed safely. We checked into Harrah's Casino and we gambled that night and the next day we rented a car to go over to Lake Tahoe. On the way over I decided we would go by the Bonanza Ranch. Bonanza was one of my favorite programs years ago. I wanted to see that big ranch. When we were going over those mountains to get over to Lake Tahoe, snow was everywhere but the roads were good. Bobbie would not let me get over twenty-five miles per hour. On the side of the road it was maybe three hundred to four hundred feet straight down. Bobbie was scared we were going to run off the road. Cars would get backed up behind me and every few miles or so, I would have to pull over on the side of the road to let them go by. I said, "Bobbie, the roads are okay, why can we not go at least forty?" She would start screaming that she was scared, so I went slowly. We finally got over the mountain and headed to the ranch and I was excited.

The ranch house sat on about five acres in the side of a mountain and across the road was Lake Tahoe. It was closed and I was very disappointed. After we got into Lake Tahoe, the snow was halfway up on cars. They had had one heck of snow. We spent the day at Lake Tahoe, and then head back to Reno. The next day we are in Harrah's gambling and Bobbie had this bracelet on and she would take and rub it over the screen of the gambling machine that she was gambling on and I would say, "Bobbie, don't do that. They will think if you win, that you have something that made you win." Bobbie said, "I'm doing this just to bring me good luck" I said okay.

We were at lunch in the restaurant there and while we were eating the head man of the casino came walking by and Bobbie said, "We are the Brannons. He said, "Yes, ma'am, we know who y'all are." Bobbie did not use the bracelet anymore. She knew what he meant. They were watching her.

We went on a trip to Thaj Maha Casino in Atlantic City. Bo Spence and his girlfriend, Darlene Sheppard, and Bobbie and I flew out of Knoxville, Tennessee. Again we were on a gambling junket and every one on this plane was a gambler. We had free flight, free rooms, and $500 free play. I do not remember the name of the airline but it was not a major airline. We flew to Atlantic City and we checked into the casino and it was very cold. We started gambling and after about twenty minutes I hit $2,500 jackpot on a twenty-five-cent red sevens machine. This was already a good trip and we gambled for a few more hours and we decided to tour the casino. It was a very big building and had lots of shops in it. While we were walking around we came up on Bo and Darlene and we asked if they wanted to have dinner with us. Bo said no, as they already had dinner. He said there was a very good restaurant in the back of the building. We decided to go in and have dinner. When we walked in through the front door water was dripping out through the top of the door and we had to dodge the water. The hostess carried us to a table and seated us. We ordered a few drinks and our dinner and just took our time enjoying our meal. Bobbie and I usually ate in a hurry because we wanted to get back gambling. That night we were laid back and took our time and enjoyed our meal. We decided it was time to leave and we paid our check and started to leave when they told us a water line had broken up stairs and the front area was closed because of the water. Now we are from the south and we have only clothes for inside the casino and we are not dressed for cold weather. They said we had to go out the back door and go about three blocks around to the front of the casino. There was just one problem, the temperature outside was -4 degrees. Bobbie and I stepped outside and we started running as hard as we could. A mugger tried to rob us but he did not catch us because of all the clothes he had on. Now you do believe that, but that was how cold it was. Next morning I turned the TV on local news and it was showing lots of apartment complexes being evacuated because of broken water pipes.

That Sunday afternoon we left the casino and headed home. After we landed in Knoxville, we got our Dodge Caravan and headed home and it was about 3:00 a.m. in the morning. We were on I-75 and just as we were about to cross the Georgia line we came up on a traffic jam. We found out two tractor trailers had wrecked and the road was closed and probably will be closed for hours. While I was sitting there I thought I saw a car go between the concrete wall that separated the northbound and southbound traffic. I got out, walked about a hundred feet to where I thought the car had gone through, and sure enough there was an opening. I walked off the opening and I thought it would be close but I believed I can make it. There was a girl sitting in a jeep in the area where I would have to get through. I walked over to the young lady and I said, "Ma'am, I am going to try and get through that opening and when I pull up here on the emergency inside lane, I would appreciate it if you would move over." She said, "sure, and if you make it, I will be behind you." I walked back to my car and walked it off and I thought you will only have inches to spare. It is around 5:00 a.m. and Bo's girlfriend had to be at work at 8:00 a.m.. I pulled up there and the young lady pulled out of the way and it took me several tries to get the car lined up to get through. Bo got out and directed me

Roy Bradie Brannon

through and I only had about two inches to spare but I made it and we went northbound, took the first exit, went over to Hwy 41, and headed south and we were on our way home.

While living in Gulf Shores, we would go over to Biloxi on occasion to gamble. We could be in Biloxi in approximately one-and-a-half hours. One Saturday, Debbie McMickle, a friend of ours, Bobbie, and I decided to go over to Beau Rivage Casino for the day and gamble. We gambled and had no luck. That afternoon we stopped to eat at their buffet. We had enough points and we did not have to pay for our meal. We ate and left and about forty-five minutes later we were headed east on I-10 going home, when all of a sudden I had got to go and I mean go. I had eaten something that had upset my stomach. There was a Mississippi rest area just ahead so I pulled into it. I had to park about 150 feet from the rest room. I got out and walked as fast as I could around a lot of people and all the time thinking I was not going to make it. Whew, I finally made it, and I walked into an empty stall, closed the door, and it flew back open. I closed it again, same thing. I moved over to the next one and about the time I was letting my pants down, I lost it. After I got through I took my underwear off, cleaned myself up the best I could, and went out to the sink and to my surprise, there was no one in there. I washed up and walked outside and started to put my shirt in my pants and, yes, I had missed a spot. I turned around to go back in and a cleaning lady was standing at the door and she said, "You cannot go in there I am fixing to clean." I said,

"Watch me I am going in." I went in took my shirt off washed it best I could put it back on and walked out and she just looked at me. I thought boy you are in for a surprise when you go in there to clean. I went around to the back of the building because there were no people around and if I had gone back the front way, I would have had to walk by a lot of people. I walked around were Bobbie could see me, which was about two hundred feet away, and I motioned for her to pull up to where I was. She pulled up in our Dodge Caravan, which had a lot of room in it. Debbie was sitting in the first back seat and I said, "Get up front." She looked at me and asked why. I said, "Don't ask questions. Get in the damn front seat," which she did. I climbed in and went to the very back to the luggage area and Bobbie said, "My god what have you done." I said, "I did not make it, turn the A/C on full blast and let all the windows down." They did and they did not argue with me. We had about thirty minutes to get to Debbie's house and it was not an enjoyable ride. When I got to Debbie's house, I took a *good* bath and borrowed a pair of her husband's pants and shirt, then we went home.

A few months later I drove over to Biloxi to the Beau Rivage Casino by myself and I got there around 6:00 p.m. and started gambling. I had lost several hundred dollars and I was down to $32.00 and I was walking, looking for a machine to play. I walked by a fifty-cent Treasure Island machine and I stopped, backed up, and I thought I have never seen one like this. I only had $32 left so I put the ticket in and started playing. I always bet the max because if you hit the jackpot and you did not bet max you win nothing. I was betting the max, I believe it was $2.50 per bet and it does not take long to eat up $32.00 dollars. I don't play a machine very long and when it got down to $16.00 I reached up to cash out and just before my hand touched the cash out button, I thought, Hey, it's 11:00 p.m. and I am tired, I will just play it out and go home. I moved my hand from the cash out button and hit max bet and all of a sudden bells and lights went off and it startled me and I wondered what I have won. At first I thought I had won $1,000. I started counting the zeros and they were way too many to be a $1,000. It finally hit me, it was $10,000, and I was very happy. I called Bobbie and told her about it and she did not believe me at first but she could tell by the excitement in my voice and she finally believed me and said, "Come home, darling my love." It took forever for them to come over and pay me. They wanted people to walk by and get excited about someone winning big time. Finally they came over and said, "Congratulations, do you want cash or check?" I said, "Check, you are not getting this back." Lucky seven's luck came through.

Later I told Bo about what I had won and a few weeks later he went down there and found the machine. Bo would bet one and then max one and then max. Well, you can guess he hit the jackpot with just one bet and did not win anything.

Roofing

My cousin David Cargle came down and we teamed up and started roofing in this area. We were working in Alabama and one of our customers wanted us to go over to Pensacola and look at her sister's house. I told her I had to be a licensed Florida roofer to work over there. She asked if I could at least give them an estimate for her insurance company. She could not get anyone to look at the roof. I said okay. We were working very close to the Florida line and it was not very far to go. I drove over to the west side of Pensacola and looked at her roof. When I got over to her house, I went up on her roof. I had never seen so many blue tarps on houses. As far as you could see in any direction you would see blue tarps on roofs. I looked at her roof and people would come up and say, "Can you look at our roof?" I called David and told him what was going on. David checked with Pensacola and they told us since this was an emergency the only requirements was you had to have workers comp insurance which we did. We started getting a lot of work, but there was a big problem, getting material and dealing with the horrible traffic jams and a place to stay. Sometime it would take an hour to go ten miles.

We started roofing a house in Pensacola and I had got the crew going and I had to leave to go look at another job. I got a call from a Florida Worker's Comp investigator who said, "I want to know if you have a permit." I said it was on the front door. The investigator said, "I need to see a copy of your insurance." I told him the owner of the company had it and he was close by and I would call and have him come over. I called David and he went right over and met with him. David showed him our Georgia worker's comp. insurance certificate. The investigator told David it was no good in Florida. He said, "Yesterday I fined a contractor $10,000 for the same thing, but you have been honest with me and I'm going to let you off. But you will have to go to an employee agency company and run your workers comp. through them. They will take out the Worker's Comp. insurance on each worker." In Florida, Worker's Comp. cost sixty-five cents on the dollar per man. If you paid a worker $100, you had to pay $65 for insurance plus other expense. It was very expensive to roof a house in Florida. There was nowhere to live in Pensacola and we finally found a cheap motel in Fairhope, Alabama, about fifty miles west of Pensacola. Later we got a cabin over there which was very nice and we stayed there for several weeks and finally, we had to move out of the cabin. When we stayed in Fairhope I would take I-10 over to Pensacola and traffic was bad and then when you got close to Pensacola it was bumper to bumper anywere you went. A section of the bridge past Pensacola was knocked out and in a short time they had rebuilt a temporary section of the damaged bridge. You could now cross the bridge but you had to go very slow. We did not need to cross the bridge but the traffic backed up for miles and miles and this was just one of our ways to get over there. You also could take US Hwy 98 and the traffic was even worse. The highway along the coast was closed and finally they opened up the beach highway and you had to have a pass to travel the road. Again they had temporally put down steel plates. You had to travel very slowly but it was faster than I-10. Finally we moved into Crystal Shores and our unit was on the eleventh floor and we were told we cannot move in. I told him we had no place to live and we were going to move in and we did. Bobbie and I got up early and headed over to Pensacola to meet the crew and roofed a house. We finished the roof and headed back home and it already was dark and we were very tired. As usual we came upon the standard roadblock but these were two new Florida sheriff deputies. They asked where we were going and I said, "Crystal Shores in Gulf Shores. We live there." He said, "Do you have proof that you live there?" I said, "No but we live there." He said, "I am sorry I cannot let you go through because you do not have a pass" Bobbie saves the day and she points to our hurricane passes taped to the front windshield. He looked at it and said, "You are free to go." We were two happy people. If they had not let us through, it would have taken at least three or four hours to get home.

I thought it will take years to roof all these houses. We went to work one day and I was driving around and there was thousands of Mexicans roofing house. One day, it was local roofers and us, and we had two crews one Mexican and a white crew we had brought down from Rome. And the next day, there were roofers everywhere.

At Crystal Shores we could only get water on the first floor, and the elevators did not work. We would take a five-gallon bucket, walk down the stairs, filled it up, and then walk back up to the eleventh floor (this reminded me of the old days). That was not fun. Sadie needed to do her thing at least three times a day and we had to walk the stairs to take her outside. Finally we had everything back to normal. Shannon had already moved in with us and she went to work for a local building supply company. After things had settled down, one weekend Bobbie and I went over to Biloxi and went gambling. Bobbie hit $2,500 jackpot. We had stayed up just about all night and came home and were very tired. We went to bed, but was so wound up we could not sleep. We got up, went to Big'O Restaurant to eat breakfast on Hwy 59 the main road through Gulf Shores to the beach. We finished our breakfast and Bobbie said we should ride down Fort Morgan

Road and look at houses. She said, "I heard if you want a house down here, that is the place to be." We drove down Ft. Morgan Road and went into several subdivisions and did not see anything we liked. We were coming back and turned right off Ft. Morgan Road on the last street before you get back to Hwy 59. We drove down E 12 Street looking at houses when we saw this house we fell in love with. The street was just before you turned left and about five blocks east was Big'O. There was a For Sale sign on the property and a gentleman was working in his yard beside the driveway. I turned into his driveway and I said, "Excuse me, what are you asking for this house?" He said, "$317,000." I said we will call the real estate agent and make an appointment to see it. He said, "Why don't you get out now and look at it?" I said, "No, we don't want to intrude on you." He said, "Get out and look at it, you won't bother us." We went through the house and it had three bedrooms, a study, Florida room with a hot tub, two full baths, dining room, nice kitchen, and the garage had a living area over the garage for Shannon and a big corner lot with lots of flowers and shrubbery. There was approximately 2,500 square feet in the house. We all walked out to the drive way and was talking when I happened to look across the street and there was Ashley car, a Ford convertible. I poked Bobbie and she said, "Wait a minute." I poked her again and she said, "What is it?" in a rude voice and I pointed across the street and Bobbie gasped and said, "Do you know who lives over there?" he said, "No, I can't remember, they just moved back in a few months ago." We were friends of their friends who lived in Rome. They would take a van and travel Tennessee and Kentucky and sell art work and they got Bruce and Ashley Johnston to do it also. The Ashley family lived just across the Tennessee line from Alabama so they had moved up there to be close to work. The friends had told us they had moved back to Gulf Shores. I said, "Bruce and Ashley." He said, "Yes, that's their name." We said okay and drove off. We looked at each other and said nope.

We rode approximately an hour looking and did not see anything we liked. Bobbie said, "Let's ride by one more time." As were pulling up to the driveway, Ashley was pulling out of her driveway which was straight across from their driveway and we all stopped. She said, "What are y'all doing here?" and Bobbie said, "We're thinking about buying this house. Will you care, Ashley?" and she said, "Heck no I am in real big hurry. Don't go anywhere. There is another one down the street you might want to look at and I will be right back."

In just a few minutes she came back and showed us the outside but we did not like it. We got to talking and she said, "Let's all go out and have a drink and celebrate yawl buying that house." That night, Bobbie, Shannon and I went out and had a few drinks with them and we all became good friends and they were very good neighbors.

We made an offer on the house and a few weeks later we moved into our new house and we loved it. After Hurricane Ivan, there was a big black cat that took up at our house in

Gulf Shores, Alabama. When I would come home, he would run and hide under one of our small buildings behind the house. After several months we would leave the back door open. He would take a tour of the house but would not let us touch him and he would go right back on his own. My son Joel came down for a visit and the first time he saw him he let Joel pick him up and he petted the cat. After that we named him Nite Nite and he became a very good pet.

We had during this time bought three more condos and we developed our own personal rental business. Customers could now rent online and pay by credit card. We were the first to allow small pets and now we were pet friendly. We were one of the first to promote pet friendliness. We had lots of repeat customers because we were pet friendly. We preferred small pets over small kids because pets do less damage. When families brought small kids, their thoughts were we were on vacation and kids had a good time and they turned them loose in our condos. What could we say? Back in our days, we said the same thing. Paybacks are hell, and what goes around comes around.

One day a lady brought five large dogs to Tradewinds during peak season and she stayed high up in the condo. Thank goodness it was not one of our condos. When she got on the elevator, no one else could get on and the children were scared and everyone else was scared of five big dogs. People complained to the condo association. After that, no pets were allowed. All good things come to an end. No more pet friendliness.

Hurricanes

The summer of 2005 was very hot and very humid and I believe this was the reason the hurricanes were so destructive. You could stand in the shade under a tree and not do anything and sweat would just pour off of you. On Monday, August 29, 2005, Hurricane Katrina hit Louisiana and this was a very destructive hurricane. This hurricane had already shut down all of the oil rigs out in the Gulf of Mexico and this disrupted the oil supply. Hurricane Katrina did only minor damage to Gulf Shores. A few weeks later Hurricane Rita hit southwestern Louisiana and affected the oil refiners in Houston, Texas, and it shut them down. The price of gas went up over four dollars per gallon. The rental business did not slow down, it came to a complete stop for approximately six months. Our condo fees went up due to insurance companies raising insurance rates because of these hurricanes and the upkeep and payments went right on. It was a tough struggle just trying to hold on to our condos. I would go back to Rome and do some roofing jobs. This helped, and we maxed out our credit cards and sold what little assets we had and it was a very hard struggle. In early 2008, my son Steve called me and asked if I would be interested in going to work by the hour and help roof the warehouse for the Floyd County Board of Education. This was a big sawtooth roof and a very big building. The warehouse had lots of leaks and I mean lots of them. I told Steve I would come up and meet with them about going to work with them. I told the Floyd County Board of Education how much per hour I wanted and what they would have to pay the roofers and laborers by the hour and we worked out an agreement. They said to get started as soon as possible.

The first person I called was Alonzo Dennis. I had worked with him over the years. I asked Alonzo if he Could come to work come work with me. Alonzo said yes. He said, "I just got fired and I am walking home." Alonzo had been drinking pretty hard the night before and at work they smelled liquor on him and they fired him. I moved into the basement of my son Sam and Cheryl house.

I put together a crew and we started in early 2008 roofing the warehouse. During this period they pulled us off and sent us up to Model high school to roof the concession stand which was north of Rome. I picked Alonzo up early every morning to go to work. In the summer we would go to work at daybreak to beat the heat. One morning I picked up Alonzo and I stopped at a convenience store in Rome to get a cup of coffee and Alonzo always got a newspaper to read. It was before 6:00 a.m. and nobody was walking anywhere around this convenience store and there was hardly any traffic. We got our coffee and newspaper and started walking out to the truck and just as we walked out the door, I saw a man standing to my right of the door. The man said, "Sir, what kind of work do you do?" I said roofing. The man said, "Do you need any help?" and I said, "No but thank you for asking." He said okay.

This stranger probably held us up for at least five seconds. Just like I said, when we pulled into this convenience store there was nobody around. We drove off and I looked at Alonzo and asked him if he found the guy strange. Alonzo said yes. We drove for approximately two miles and as I was going past the Floyd County Jail and we were going down a small hill. I could see what I thought was fog at the bottom of the hill. I thought to myself where did that fog come from because we had not seen any fog anywhere else. I slowed down as we got to what I thought was fog, it was smoke coming from a turned over tractor and trailer. We got completely beside it before I realized it was a big truck turned over on the side of the road. Alonzo and I got out and ran around to the cab of the truck and, I hollered, "Is there anyone in there?" A man hollered out yes. I asked, "Are you hurt?"

He said, "No, but what about the car I hit?"

I said, "Oh my goodness, you must be on top of the car."

I ran around the truck to see if he was on top of a car. You got to remember when we first arrived there was so much smoke you could hardly even see the truck. I ran back around to the driver and I said, "You didn't hit a car," and he said, "Yes, I did."

About that time people came walking down from the intersection which was about six hundred or seven hundred feet away and the driver said to them, "Did I hit a car"? And they said, "Yes, you hit a car but nobody was hurt." I believe the driver went to sleep and he was probably going eighty miles or more per hour when he hit the car and it woke him up. He turned over on the driver's side and slid approximately seven hundred feet down the northbound lane. He had turned over on the driver's side and his truck was sliding in the diesel fuel that was spilling out. This was what was causing all the smoke. If it had been gasoline there probably would have been no truck left. If it had not been for my guardian angel that delayed me for about five seconds, I would probably have been mixed up in this wreck. This was a very close call and I do now believe in guardian angels.

We started back roofing on the warehouse and my lunch every day I would eat a six-inch tuna whole wheat bread sandwich and water, eating what I thought was healthy. About one hour later I would have to find a shady spot on the roof to lie down and take a short nap. I wondered why I got so sleepy everyday like this. I thought it was because I was getting older. I went to see my regular doctor Keith

Palmer. He took a small stick and punched my legs through my socks. Dr. Palmer asked, "Do you feel this?" I said just a little bit. Dr. Palmer said, "I bet your sugar averages 180." I said yes. He said, "If you don't get it under control you are in real trouble." What he was trying to say was if I didn't get it under control, odds were I was going to lose my legs. That really scared me, and I really started looking for ways to control my sugar. Doctor Palmer told me, "Don't eat anything white, potato chips or sweets."

I was watching CNN when this health food lady said to be aware of foods that are sugar-free. They contain corn syrup and it is worse than sugar. And she also said, "If you eat a salad at restaurants, you would be better off eating a double whopper burger." She said, "Beware of the salad dressings that you use." I started watching what was in salad dressings and I read the labels and it surprised me what's in them. My sugar was getting a little better and the average was around 150. I was making progress but I could not get it below 150.

Bobbie was living in Gulf Shores, Alabama, taking care of the condos and she was doing a good job. I would not go home very often because I could not afford the gas to travel back to Gulf Shores. It would cost about $225 round trip. I was working at the Floyd County Board of Education roofing their warehouse and we could only work forty hours per week. And on the weekends I would do other roofing jobs. I was working seven days a week trying to keep the ship from sinking.

Due to the situation in Gulf Shores, my credit was ruined and Charles Griffin, my real estate agent, told me about a house that my bank had reprocessed and Greater Rome Bank was ready to get this house off of their books. On October 6, 2008, Charles and I went by and looked at this house. It was in very good location in East Rome and it was a three-bedroom, one bath upstairs and one bath downstairs in the unfinished basement. The house had fourteen steps up in the front and fourteen steps up in the basement. I told Charles I wanted it because this was probably my only chance to buy a home in Rome because of my bad credit. I told Charles what I would give for the house and he called my banker, David Mullinax, and made the offer. David said yes, I could have the house. The next morning, October 7, I went to work and we were installing GAF Liberty MB peel and stick roll roofing. This saw tooth roof I was working on was not steep but it had a good slope to it and at the bottom edge of the roof there was a valley and a wall above the valley so you could not fall off the roof. The material we used you would set the roll in place and you would pull the plastic film out from under the roll and it would stick to the base sheet. Base sheet was a material that we nailed down first before we installed the MB. When you put the last roll of MB down for the day you would leave the three-inch strip of plastic film on the lap for the next day. You would remove the three-inch film when you put the next roll on the next day. It was October 7, 2008, and about 8:30 a.m. in the morning and there was morning dew on the roof. I was walking across the roof and looking back talking to someone when I stepped on the three-inch wet strip and my feet went out from under me and I fell hard, straight down on the roof on my right leg. I knew I had broken it and I said, "I have broken my leg." Alonzo said, "I doubt it, you probably just bruised it." I knew my leg was broken and I got on my cell phone and called 911. The roof on this warehouse was very long and only had a side entrance to the roof. I was about a hundred feet from the edge of the roof and thank goodness, this job was not far away from emergency stations. Dustin Roser, one our workers, asked, "Do you want me to go out front and direct the emergency vehicles back here?" and I said yes. We were working in the back section of this warehouse and it would've been hard to find. It was not long before they had arrived—firemen, EMTs, and ambulance personnel were up on the roof. They loaded me on a stretcher, strapped me in, and carried me over to the edge of the roof. They secured me on the end of a ladder the fire truck had sent up to the edge of the roof. They let me down and put me in the ambulance. On the way to the hospital the ambulance seemed like it hit every bump there was in the road and when it started down Turner McCall Boulevard and all of a sudden they had to lock it down and I thought, *Oh my God, now we are going to be involved in a wreck.*

When we got to Floyd Hospital, the ambulance drivers lifted me up to put me on a hospital bed. The pain was unbearable. I rose up screaming. One of the ambulance attendance hollered, "Lay down." He was very, very rude to me and I told Floyd Hospital about his behavior and they said they would check into it.

I lay on the hospital table and they came in to x-ray my leg. They folded two towels and put them up under my leg to raise my leg off the table. At the time I knew my leg was broken but I did not know exactly where the break was. It was broken just above my ankle and they placed the towels up just past the break and my foot was hanging over the towels and it was very painful. I was hollering for them to hurry. Finally they got through with the x-rays and I asked the nurse who was taking care of me in the emergency room, "It's bad, isn't it?" The nurse said, "I cannot say anything. You have to wait until the doctor comes in." I said, "You don't have to say anything, I can see it in your face. Things don't look good." By this time I had already had a morphine shot and I was not feeling much pain. Soon the doctor came in and said, "You have a bad break." He showed me the x-rays and it was not a clean break. It was a zigzag break just above my ankle. Dr. Sand asked me when was the last time I have had anything to eat. I said, "Last night I have not had breakfast this morning. I usually eat breakfast every morning." He said, "That is good we going to take you on up for surgery," and they did.

The break on the backside of my leg had an open gap in the break and to me it looked like an eighth of an inch. They operated and drove a rod from my knee to my ankle and put two screws below my knee and two screws just above my ankle. Dr. Sands said if the rod had not been installed in the old days I would have been laid up on my back in traction for at least fifteen weeks. He said, "It's going to take three to six months to get you well." I was put in a private room. I took pain medicine every four hours and on the second night I got up to go to the bathroom and hobbled into the bathroom on my walker. I sat down on the commode and did my thing. I stood up to pull my underwear up and I was on pain medicine and could only stand on one leg. As I tried to pull my underwear up, I lost my balance and I almost fell. I sat back down and pushed the emergency button and the nurse came in and I said, "I have my modesty, but now I don't care what you see." The nurse said, "Don't you ever do that again. It is our job and we don't think anything about it."

The next day I was in pain and I complained to the nurse on duty and she said, "I'll take care of you." She gave me a shot of morphine. A few minutes later, three pretty young physical therapists came in and said I had to get up and walk the hall on my walker. I said to them, "Y'all will have to come back later. Right now I'm on cloud nine and when I land you can take me walking." It was not long after I landed they came back and got me up and it was hard walking with a bad leg on that walker. If it had not been for those three ladies, I don't think I could have made it down the hall and back. I stayed in the hospital for four days and then went to stay in my son's basement. The bedroom in the basement was very close to a bathroom and I had a little hot oven and small refrigerator and I could take care of myself pretty good.

Bobbie was still in Gulf Shores, Alabama, taking care of our six condos and that kept her very busy. After a week in my son's basement, I wanted to go home and let my baby help take care of me. Charles and his son, Charlie, carried me to Montgomery, Alabama, to meet with Shannon and Michael Selby. Charles had made me a bed in the back of his vehicle and the trip was not that bad. I had to lay flat with my leg elevated or it would swell up pretty bad. I got home and stayed a week but I had to go back to Rome to take the stitches out. We had a Dodge Caravan and I could travel in it a lot better than traveling in a car. After we saw Dr. Sands and he took the stitches out, we then headed to Athens, Alabama. Bobbie's mom and dad lived in Athens, about 150 miles from Rome. They lived on the Tennessee River close to Wheeler dam. The water was three miles wide in front of their house which was very close to the water and it was a very nice. I would lie on the couch and I would say, "Bobbie, would you get me something to drink?" and she would say, "I'm not waiting on you get up and get it yourself." I would ask Freddie, Bobbie's brother, and he would say the same thing. I would have to lay around with my leg elevated to help keep it from swelling. They would say, "You need to exercise that leg," and I thought how in the hell can I carry something to drink on a walker.

After a few days in Athens, Alabama, we headed home to Gulf Shores. We arrived at our house which was just one mile from the beach. This house was very nice. It had four bedrooms, two baths and over the garage one bedroom and one bath. It was on a large corner lot and we were very close to downtown Gulf Shores. We had been home for about thirty minutes and I had gotten in bed because I needed to lie down and elevate my leg because traveling was hard on me. I was lying in the bed and Bobbie started screaming, "Help, help!"

I got out of bed and went as fast as I could on my walker to see what was wrong. Bobbie was sitting on the floor in the main bathroom and the waterline under the sink had broken at the cutoff and Bobbie was holding her fingers on it to slow the water down. This house was built on a concrete slab and we had lots of nice carpet in the house. We were lucky that we had tile on the bathroom floor. I called 911 and said we had a broken water line in the house and I've got a broken leg and I cannot do anything. The 911 operator said, "I am sending you an ambulance," and I said, "No, no, I broke it a few weeks ago and I'm on a walker." The 911 operator said, "Okay, I will connect you to the fire department." Luckily the fire department was only approximately ten blocks away. I told the fire department our problem and we needed help as soon as possible and he said they were on their way. I hobbled out to the front porch and the fire department arrived a few minutes later. I pointed to the area where I thought the water meter was and yes I forgot to say it was very dark outside. The leaves had fallen in over the water meter and they had a hard time finding it and after they found it they opened the lid to the water meter and yes, it was full of sand, and finally they got the sand out and cut the water off. Bobbie was not mad but maybe a little mad because water had spewed all over her and she did not look good when the four good looking young firemen came in. These firemen were very nice. They pitched in and helped clean up the mess. Thank goodness the water stayed in the bathroom area. From then on when we would come back to Rome to see the doctor, we would cut the water off. If we had been out of town when that water line broke, our house would have been destroyed.

Our bedroom was in the back of the house and it was a long way off from the kitchen. I would have to lie in bed and keep my leg elevated to keep it from swelling. I would say, "Bobbie, would you get me a cup of coffee," and she would say, "I'm not waiting on you, get up and get it yourself. You need to exercise that leg." Once I tried to get a cup of coffee myself and I think I had about half a cup left by the time I got to my bed. After about eight weeks we went back to Rome (water off) to see Dr. Sands. They x-rayed my leg and he came in the room where I was and Dr. Sands showed me the x-ray and said, "You are not healing."

I said, "What do you mean I am not healing?"

He showed me the x-ray again and pointed out that on the backside of my leg the break was still open. Dr. Sands said, "I told you it would take three to six months to get you well, I'm going to try something on your leg. I want you to go to another room and a young man will show you how to use a small gadget on your leg."

The young man came in and strapped a small gadget over the broken area. He said, "This will shoot electrons into your leg and it should cause the bone to heal." He told me to do this two times a day, twenty minutes each time, for eight weeks.

In 2008, Earl had a stroke and was in Floyd Hospital and I went by in a wheelchair to see him. He seemed okay and in good spirits and I thought he was going to be okay. Bobbie and I left and headed back to Gulf Shores, Alabama. Earl had another stroke and he was in bad shape. Willard, my nephew, was taking care of him. Earl was dying and he told Willard, "Take me home to die." Willard said, "Okay, I will take you home." The hospital said if he took Earl home, he was going to die. Willard told them that was where he wanted to die and he was taking him home. Earl was bedridden. Willard and his sons took good care of Earl. Later I visited him at his house and he said, "That was a big mistake coming home. I wish I had stayed and died." Earl lived a miserable life and several years later he died.

When Dr. Sands told me the bad news I knew that it would be a long time before I could go back to work. I went back to Gulf Shores called an attorney and filed for Chapter 7 bankruptcy. Later I went back to see Dr. Sands and I had high hopes that electrons worked. He came into the room and said he had bad news. "It did not work." I was very disappointed and he said, "I am going to take the rod out and drill your leg bone out to your ankle and reinstall the rod."

I thought this sounded bad but I had no choice. A few days later I was admitted to Floyd Hospital and they did the operation. A few days later I went home to Gulf Shores. Approximately eight weeks later, I came back to Rome to see Dr. Sands and I went to a room to wait and see what he was going to say. I was very nervous and wondering if this does not work what's next. After what seemed likes hours, he came in and said, "When we drilled the bone out the bone marrow had settled into the broke area and now you are healed and you can go back to work." This was very late 2008 and on March 29, 2009, we went before the bankruptcy judge and it was final. After we had filed bankruptcy in 2008, Bobbie moved to the house I had bought in Rome and I stayed in Gulf Shores until everything was finalized. Around the first of April I got a friend of mine to load our TVs and other things on a trailer I had bowered from Keith Morris. Late that afternoon I headed to Rome. I was about to cross the Georgia line and I was thinking when I get to LaGrange I was going to stop stretch and get me something to drink and plug up my cell phone. When I crossed into Georgia, and in front of the new Kia plant, a tire blew out on the trailer. I was about twenty miles from LaGrange. There was just enough room to pull off on the side of I-85 interstate. Traffic was flying by about eighty miles an hour, and I was thinking about what I was going to do. I get on my cell phone, which had very little battery life left because while traveling I was not able to reach my charger. It was about 8:00 p.m. Sunday night, and I called information and asked for information for tire store and they gave me a number. I called it and they said they were about fifty miles away and there was nothing they could do. I was thinking I was going to get killed on this road so I started to call 911 but I had to wait until my phone charged. My phone had gone completely dead and I had to wait for what seemed like forever to make the call. Finally I had enough power and I called 911 and I said, "Can you connect me with the Georgia State Patrol," and they did. I told the Georgia State Patrol my problem and they said, "We will have someone out very soon." A trooper arrived and I told him my problem and he said, "I know of someone in Lagrange, Georgia, that's not that far away. Do you want me to call them?" It was not long afterward a wrecker showed up and he disconnected the trailer and pulled it up on his wrecker and he said, "I will take you to Walmart and they should be able to help you." It was close to 10:00 p.m. when we got to Walmart and they have just closed the tire repair section for the night. The wrecker driver said, "If you will buy a tire I will put it on for you," and I said, "okay let's do it." Well, there was one problem, the person who sold the tires and had the keys had gone to eat and they could not find him. About an hour later we finally got the tire. Well now it even gets better, the wrecker driver gets a call and he has to go close to Columbus, Georgia, on a service call which was about fifty miles away. He told me they were on AAA emergency calls and he had to go on this call. He said, "Follow me home and I will drop off your trailer at my house and when I get through I will fix your tire." I follow him home and he unloaded the trailer and headed out. I sit in my truck for about two hours and later he returns and fixes my tire. Now another problem developed, it began to start drizzling and the TVs and everything were exposed to the rain. He found a big outside umbrella and we strapped it to the trailer and about 2:00 a.m. I head out hoping for the best. I travel to Rome and only hit light rain here and there and just as I pull into my driveway around 5:00 a.m. it began to rain hard and I pulled up under a shed and now everything was in the dry. I was tired and gave out and glad to be home.

On April 10, 2009, Nite and I packed up for the last and final time and headed to Rome. After I got past Montgomery late in the afternoon, Bobbie called me and said, "It's storming here, where are you?" I said, "No storms, the sun is shining and it is clear." About thirty minutes later she would call again, "We're having storms here," and she was keeping our little granddaughter Gracie Byars. Not long after that she called again and said, "Gracie and I are headed to the basement, it is really bad here." At this time I did not see any bad clouds but when I got to Lagrange, Georgia, it looked bad north of Lagrange, and after I got through Lagrange, I had my radio on and now I was headed into no man's land. What I mean by that was there were no stores or nothing, nowhere to take shelter. After I got a few miles north of Lagrange, and I was very close to Franklin, Georgia, it came over the radio tornado spotted over Franklin. US 27 was now a four-lane highway and the new four lane had bypassed the small towns. It now was now no man's land. Yes, I was scared and I looked off to the east toward Atlanta and I could see the tornado in the air just off to my right. Thank goodness it was not on the ground and it had just passed over Hwy 27 in front of me. Yes, I was very nervous driving north in this stormy weather. Just as I got approximately ten miles south of Cedartown, I went into the storm and it was raining so hard I had to pull over and stop. All this time I was thinking if there was a tornado in this storm and my luck was with me, no tornado.

Late 2009, Sam called and said, "Cheryl and I have never been to Las Vegas. Can you go and get us some rooms?"

I said, "Sam I don't know if I will be able."

Sam said, "You have been there lots times and you know what to do."

I said, "Okay, let me see what I can do." I called Harrah's Casino and got us rooms. Before we left to go to Las Vegas, I went by Dr. Sand's office and picked up a letter. I had him write me a letter about rods and pins in my leg. I had heard horror stories of people going through metal detectors. We get to Atlanta Airport and I walk through metal detector, throw my hand up, and I said, "Search me."

The lady looked at me and asked, "Why do you want us to search you?"

I said, "I have rods in my leg."

She said, "I will search you if you really want me to."

She was smiling at me like I really wanted her to. I said, "No, that is okay."

We then flew to Las Vegas. After a couple of days we rented a car drove over to see the Hoover Dam. Bobbie and I had already seen it several times. We still enjoyed seeing it. Sam and Cheryl were very impressed at seeing it. We left and on the way back we stopped at a small casino close to Hoover Dam. There was hardly anyone in there. I played the slots. Bobbie, Sam, and Cheryl played the dice tables for the first time. They had a very good time playing the dice tables. They were screaming and laughing and having a good time. The casino treated us to lunch. That was the best time of our gambling trip. We left and went back to Las Vegas. We had tickets to go to the Venetian and go hear and see the Jersey Boys.

Sam said, "You want me get a taxi?"

I said, "No, it is only a few blocks from us."

We walked down to the Venetian and go in and asked, "Where is the Jersey Boys show?"

To my surprise, the lady said, "Go that way, it is in the very back of the casino."

We walked about another three blocks. We went in and walked up to the desk to get our tickets which Cheryl had bought online. Our seats were way back and I was cutting up with the young lady behind the desk. The young lady said, "I am going to move y'all to the second row." We had not mentioned nothing about our seats. It was the lucky seventh son that made it happen. We had the best seats in the house. That was the best show we had ever seen. We headed back to our hotel and it was all I could do to make it back. I thought any minute my leg was going to lock up on me. We left and flew back to Atlanta. We went to pick up our luggage. Bobbie was loaded down with luggage, and Sam was helping out with the luggage. We were walking down the hall and I was not carrying anything. A man walks by and said, "Why don't you help this lady with her luggage?" Sam said, "Why don't you mind your on damn business?" We just kept walking. I wonder what people thought about Bobbie loaded down and me nothing. I bet it was not good.

I went back to work and at first everything was great but few weeks later I started having trouble with my ankle. The break was just above my ankle but there were two screws very close to my ankle. Dr. Sands decided to operate and take those two screws out. This was my third operation and after the two screws were removed my ankle was okay. About three months later, I was having very sharp pains in the area where I broke my leg. I went back to see Dr. Sands, and he said, "I have done all I can do." And he made me an appointment with Dr. Douglas Lundy at Kennastone Hospital in Kennesaw, Georgia, about fifty miles east of Rome.

I went to see Dr. Lundy and he decided to take the rod out and install a plate on the side of my leg. Late May 2010, operation number four, Dr. Lundy operated on my leg, removing the screws and the rod. I went back later for a Preopp and he told me what he was going to do. He was going to take a bone graft out of my leg above my knee to use it on the break area. I went back on August 19, 2010, and Dr. Lundy operated and installed a plate, approximately 1"x 7" on the side of my leg with lots of screws in the plate. Dr. Lundy went into my knee to get the bone graft. This was number five. At first everything looked good but later the pain started again in the area of the break. I made an appointment to see Dr. Lundy. I went back to his office and he x-rayed my leg. He said everything looked good but that I could be allergic to titanium. Dr. Lundy said he had a patient and when he saw a rash on him he knew he was allergic to titanium. I said, "Dr. Lundy, I had two bad rashes on my leg I had to go to a dermatologist and it took a year to clear it up."

"Yes," he said, "that's what it sounds like, but it's too early to operate now."

In late April I could not stand the pain so I made an appointment for May 12, 2011, to take the plate out. The pain got so bad I called and said I couldn't wait until the twelfth so they rescheduled the operation for May 4, 2011. This was operation number six. Dr. Lundy operated and the plate was removed and I woke up in recovery and the nurse told me my blood pressure was going up and I was on the verge of a stroke. The nurse was panicking and I still had the I-don't-care medicine in me and I thought to myself, *I don't give a damn*. She would check my blood pressure every few minutes and my blood pressure would be up. She would call someone and give me a shot. I believe my blood pressure had peaked at about 200 and then started going slowly back down. If I had not had the medicine in me, I would probably have panicked like she did and I would probably had a stroke. I stayed in Kennastone Hospital for three days. While I was in the hospital, they installed a Novocain pump on my leg.

When we got home to Rome, Bobbie used a wheelchair to get me in the house. Thank goodness we had a side deck that was only about a foot high off the ground and after I broke my leg, Charles built a ramp to the deck. Bobbie rolled me into the bedroom beside my bed and I stood up on my good leg and sat back on the bed. I lifted my good leg onto the bed. Then I tried to lift my right leg and it would not move. I could not lift the right leg because it was numb from the Novocain and it felt like it weighed a hundred pounds. Bobbie had to lift my leg up on the bed. If I had to get up to go to the bathroom, Bobbie would have to lift my leg up. Three days later, at about 5:00 a.m., I woke up screaming. "Bobbie, you gotta do something! I've got sharp pains in my knee area." I said, "Get the scissors and cut this Ace bandage off of me," because the pain was unbearable. The Novocain pump was out and the feeling had come back. They had wrapped my leg too tight where you bend your leg, especially on the backside of my leg, and it looked like I had been cut several times. We called Dr. Lundy's office and they said for us to comedown to his office. We did not see Dr. Lundy, another doctor rewrapped my leg. Bobbie's friend, Shane Jackson, who she had worked with at Applebee's, told her later Dr. Lundy chewed out the person who wrapped my leg. Shane was Dr. Lundy's assistant in the operating room and two weeks later I went back to see Dr. Lundy to get the stitches out. Dr. Lundy told Bobbie and me that he gave up on getting the titanium plate off of my leg. He told his assistant to get it off, and his assistant took a hammer and chiseled it off my leg. No wonder why they installed a Novocain pump on my leg.

After I recovered from my sixth operation, I went to the Floyd County Hospital Rehabilitation Center in West Rome. John Goodrich was my physical therapist and when I first started, I was in bad shape. I went to physical therapy three times a week and after a few weeks I asked John what the odds were of me getting better, and he said about 10 percent. After months of therapy, I got a lot better and I was released to go back to work even though I could only walk a very short distance. I could only stand for just a few minutes and I could not squat down.

Deteriorating Health

My health was going downhill. My sugar was around 150, and I had arthritis in my knees and shoulders. I cannot raise my arms above my head and touch them together. As Shag would say, "Swannee I just about had the lick." I had high blood pressure and my cholesterol was high. I had a bad case of sinus drainage and when I got out of my chair I had to climb out of it. And when I went downstairs, I had to walk sideways and hold on. If there was no rail, I could not go downstairs. One day Bobbie was cutting grass at our home and she said, "You need to help me." I got the weed eater out and started using it. I used the weed eater for about fifteen to twenty minutes and I had to quit. I lay in bed for several days with a swollen leg. I have an old duplex on Maple Road that I was fixing up and I used a step ladder to trim the ceiling. When I finished my leg started hurting and I lay in bed again for three days with a swollen leg. After that we got Alunzo Dennis to come over and help Bobbie cut the grass. Bobbie said, "Alunzo, look at him, he is useless. He's not good for anything." That hurt bad but it was true. One night I went over to Georgia Highland college gym to watch the Pepperell High School girls play basketball. Pepperell had a very good girls' basketball team and they were exciting to watch. At the end of the gym, they had rails to hold on to and I used the rails to go up to find me a seat. The next night I went to see them play again and there was a long line and I had to stand in line to get my tickets. This was not fun. It was hard on my leg and I finally got in the gym and it was full. People were already sitting next to the rail so I had to go up a section with no rails to get a seat. I could go up, but I could not come down without assistance. I just went up to the fourth set of bleachers to get a seat. I thought I could make it back down without much trouble and just before the end of the game, I thought you had better get out of here before the crowd starts to leave. I stood up to go down when it hit me I can't go down without help. What am I going to do? The bleacher steps were deep and my knee was weak. My right ankle was stiff. I would need something to hold onto because coming down the bleachers you had to take long steps which I could not do. I finally started down. I would ask the person sitting next to the aisle, "Excuse me, could I put my hand on your shoulder?" I told them I had a bad leg and I had to have support to get down. They all let me do it and I got down okay. Due to my injury my ankle was stiff and going down those bleachers my right ankle would not bend and let me step down. I never tried that again.

I would take Bobbie to Walmart and I would sit in the car because I could not walk through Walmart, my leg would start hurting. As I sat in the car I would watch the people walk by and it seemed like 75 percent of the people who came by was overweight or obese and you could tell some had bad knees. I know I had bad knees. In early May 2012, I was thinking my health was so bad that I felt like a ninety-year-old invalid. I thought I was gradually dying and I was about ready to throw in the towel and die. I thought, *Old lucky seven, your luck has run out.* I was seventy-two years old and almost an invalid. My blood pressure was very high, my cholesterol was high, and my sugar was high. I slept with a Kleenex box in bed with me. If I had to make a choice the Kleenex box or my wife Bobbie, I'd had to take the Kleenex box because my sinus drainage was horrible. I was lucky if I slept two hours a night. On Thursday, May 19, 2012, I heard about the book *Wheat Belly* by Dr. William Davis. I said to myself what have I got to lose and I ordered the book that day and I received it three days later. I began reading the book as soon as I got it. I started eating good healthy foods, lots of vegetables and fruits. I cut way back on meats and I completely eliminated wheat from my diet plus lots of other foods. The first five days were the hardest. I was craving bread so bad I almost gave in, but after that it got better. I took Dr. Davis's advice and I eliminated all processed foods, Coke, milk, and juices. I now drink lots of water. I started searching and reading good healthy books. I turned my life completely around thanks to healthy foods. I was taking two metaform pills in the morning and two at night for my diabetes. Every morning I could not wait to check my sugar. Late every afternoon I would check my sugar. Every time I checked it my sugar it was down. This was exciting to see my health improving. Three weeks later, I cut my medicine for my diabetes in half and six weeks later, I cut it out completely. After a few weeks I sat down to eat a good healthy meal and my wife brought me a big glass of milk. I said, "Why did you bring me that big glass of milk?" Bobbie said, milk was good for me and I needed to drink it. The next morning I checked my sugar and it was 150 and I wondered what caused the spike as I ate a good healthy meal the night before. I decided to check the milk and it showed 11 percent sugar. After that, no more milk.

Later I was watching CNN and this lady was talking about healthy foods and she said be leery of food that say NO SUGAR as they will have corn syrup in them and that was worse than sugar. I really started reading labels after that. I started working out in Floyd Rehab Center. Once you are a patient you can go back and work out free. Before I read the book *Wheat Belly*, my weight was 181 pounds and I am now down to 162 pounds. My waist went from 36 inches to 34 inches. In June I went to a family reunion in Cave Spring George and I told my son Sam and his wife Cheryl about what I was doing. She said she could not do that. She went on a diet and got to craving carbohydrate so bad she had to come off of her diet. I told her this was not a diet, you can eat all the good food you want and you will lose weight. Dr. William Davis said, "There is no diet that works because your craving for carbohydrates will take over and you will give in." I know since then people have improved their diets. Since I gave up wheat and processed foods, my sinus drainage is 90 percent gone. Now I sleep all night. After about three months, Bobbie and I went to Chili's for dinner. Bobbie told the server she wanted hot wings. The server asked if we wanted the boneless or the ones with bones. I asked for the boneless. We ate our dinner and our hot wings and then we went home. Later we went to bed and I tried to go to sleep. Something turned the faucet on in my head and my sinus drainage was horrible and I may have slept two hours that night at most. About 5:00 a.m., it hit me what the problem was. The boneless wings were processed. The wings with bones in them were not processed, they were frozen. I have always thought frozen food was not good. They are better because the good ingredients are frozen in.

In early June, I went back to Cave Spring to the Arts and Crafts Festival. I saw a friend of mine, Mike Ragland, who was a retired major with the city of Rome police. Mike was at a booth selling his book *Bertha*. *Bertha* is a very interesting book to read and if you start reading the book it will be hard to put it down. I asked him how he was doing, and he said he was pretty good. Mike was a big man and overweight. I was going to tell him about the book but I changed my mind and turned, took about two steps, and I stopped, then I thought, *What the hell.* I went back and told Mike. I said, "Mike, there is a book you need to read called *Wheat Belly*, and it has really helped me." Mike wrote it down. A few months later, I called Mike to check and see if he had bought the book. Mike said, that after I told him about the book, a few days later, he was watching Bill O'Reilly and he had recommended this book. He said that two people had mentioned this book to him, somebody was trying to tell him something. He bought the book. Mike said he could not walk to the end of his driveway because he would be out of breath. He has lost weight and now walks five miles a day. This made me feel very good.

My health began to really improve and I went over to Barron Stadium, a football stadium, where Rome High School plays its football games. I walked three times around the football field and later I walked six times around and I was very proud. This made me feel very good now I could walk about anywhere I wanted too. I could now touch my hands together over my head and I don't have to go down stairs sideways. I had brown spots on my arms and I wore long sleeve shirts because I was a shamed of those brown spots. Now those brown spots are gone. I had eczema around my nose and now it is gone. I am not limited to how far I can walk I feel now like a sixty-year-old man and I feel great. Due to my bad leg, I cannot do any physical labor or stand on my bad leg very long. I cannot squat down I have to be very careful where I walk because my knee was weak due to all of those surgeries on my right leg.

Medicine Free

In September 2013, I went to see Dr. Palmer and saw his assistant, Ashley Millican, NP. They checked my blood pressure and it was 118/60, very good. They drew lots of blood to test and one week later the nurse, Kim, called me and said, "Everything came back normal!" That was great news, and now I am medicine free. I can now touch my hands over my shoulder. The arthritis in my knees is now gone. I don't have to climb out of my chair. I can hold my arms straight up and stand straight up. Several months before this I had gradually cut back on my cholesterol and blood pressure medicine. I am medicine free. This old lucky seven is back. You must lead yourself to good health. My regular foods I eat for breakfast is an egg omelet with onions, tomatoes, and mushrooms. For lunch and dinner, I eat spinach and romaine lettuce, onions, tomatoes, mushroom, cucumbers, blueberries, walnuts, and homemade ranch dressing. Also I eat wild caught salmon and Purdue range fed chicken with no hormones in them and all natural foods. I do not eat chickens with hormones and other chemicals in them. You will develop your own good foods to eat. Everyone has a different taste. When I started doing my thing, there wasn't a lot of choices that you could find in the supermarkets. Today, Kroger's has a fresh vegetables and fruit sections to pick from. Kroger also has a lot of organic foods and a selection of good foods in their cooler section. Kroger now has EZEKIEL 4:9 original-flourless low glycemic bread. Kroger now has a meat section of good natural meats to eat. When I say natural I mean no GMO's in them. In my opinion, Kroger's is number one in healthy foods.

When I was young you we had a Murrieta bakery in Rome. At night they baked their bread and every morning shipped it out to the stores. They would pick up the bread they had delivered the day before. They would bring the bread back and sell it next door as day-old bread. Today a friend of mine picked up a loaf of bread and they said it had on the wrapper To Be Used in 16 Days. Real bread will last about three or four days. It is not loaded with chemicals and preservatives. I no longer eat crackers made from wheat. I eat almond, brown rice, and sesame seed crackers. In the old days almost all cities had a local bakery. Do you read the calories or do you read the chemicals in food? Remember to read the labels. You must lead yourself to good health.

In the summer of 2013, Bobbie saw an ad in the *Rome News Tribune* that said you pick three gallons, and you keep two gallons of blueberries. I eat blueberries every day they are very good for you. She called and got directions one early Saturday morning. We headed out to pick blueberries. We got to his house and he tells us that he will take us across the road. We parked our car and waited for him to take us down to the blueberry patch. We were east of Rome and we were way out in the country. I said, "We are not far from Bartow county," and he said, "You turn left out of my driveway and you are in Bartow County." We drove across and parked in this very clean open field. And we got out and he carried us about three hundred feet down this trail with broom sage and bushes on each side of the trail. He showed us the blueberry patch and said, "Go to it."

We picked blueberries for about three hours and filled up six buckets. Bobbie and I started back down the trail and as usual Bobbie is dragging behind. I was walking down this big trail when I noticed something moving on the trail. I walk on up to see what was moving on the trail and to my surprise it was a big rattlesnake. Bobbie was about a hundred feet behind, and I said, "Bobbie get up here, I just seen a big rattlesnake." Bobbie came running up. She said, "You have seen what?"

I said, "A big rattle snake."

"Where?" I pointed in the broom sage where it went. Bobbie said, "Let's get out of here."

We were walking very fast down the trail headed to our car. When we were not far from our car, and at the end of the trail, and just as we stepped out into the open field, I looked to my left and there lay a large rattlesnake about six feet away. It looked about five feet long and I took a step to my right to get away from it. There was a hog wire metal gate lying on the ground. I don't even take one good step when I fall down on this gate. Well, Bobbie was scared and ran, jumped in the car, left, and came back about thirty minutes later to see if I was dead. Just kidding. I am laying there and with my bad leg I could not get up fast. With my bad leg it was very slow getting up by myself. Bobbie came right back, and helped me get up. I turned and looked for the snake and thank goodness he was gone. He was probably as scared of us as we were of him. I spilled very little of my berries and we gathered them up and got out there. We went back to his house and told the owner what happened and he said let me get my shotgun and let's go back. We went back and found the snake and he killed it and it was at least five feet long. If it had bitten me that far out I would never have made it back to Rome. We now pick our berries at Kroger.

I was at Kroger's in summer of 2013 shopping when I ran into a friend of mine, Judy Evans. Judy said, "Hi, Roy, you look so different, what have you done?"

I said, "I do feel great."

"Yes, you do, and you look like you feel good. What did you do? I want to know."

I pointed at her buggy and said, "I don't eat that and that," and I pointed to about 75 percent of everything in her buggy.

Judy said, "Most of it are for the grandchildren. They're coming over for the weekend."

I said you need to get the book *Lose the Wheat Lose the Weight* by Dr. William Davis. Also I told Judy to get the book *Eat to Live* by Joel Fuhrman, MD. Those were two good books to read.

Judy said, "Where can I get those books?"

"Barnes and Noble," which was in the same shopping center. Judy left Kroger and went straight to Barnes & Noble and bought those books. Judy's husband, Larry Evans, also read the book and on December 13, 2013, I saw him and he had lost eight pounds and two inches off his waist. Larry was not overweight but was a tall, big man. He said he had a stroke a few years back and his left leg had hurt him ever since. When he went wheat free, a few weeks later the pain went away. I asked how Judy was doing and he said, "she was doing great and she was wheat free."

Around December 1, 2013, I called Mike Ragland and asked him how he was doing and he said he had gone to see his doctor for a checkup. Mike told me he was shocked at what his doctor told him. Everything was not good and now he had to go and have stress tests. Mike told me he had gone back to his old ways of eating and was now paying the price. Mike said he was going back to eating healthy foods. You know medicine has side effects and if you see their ads on TV, you should be scared to take their medicine. I told friends of mine, Les and Tammy Groves, what I was doing right after I started doing my thing. A couple of months ago I saw Les at the Ace Hardware in Lindale and he said he was now wheat free. Les said he had lost eighteen pounds and felt great. I asked about Tammy and he said she was also wheat free.

The week of December 16, 2013, I heard on the news that beer sales were down. I wondered why, beer was made from wheat. There's one beer that I know of, Red Bridge, that has no wheat in it. I don't drink beer, I drink a little rum, which is also wheat free. I saw on the Internet about the five worst foods and wheat was number one and second was orange juice. And just a few months back I heard on the news that orange juice sales had fallen off.

I believe people are waking up. Like I said earlier, when I had to sit in the car at Walmart or any other stores, and I observed people walking by, I could see the discomfort in their faces and the majority were overweight and they looked like they felt bad. When you're in that shape you can't hide it. I know this because I have been there. Judy knew I felt great, she could see it in my face. Are you trying to hide how you really feel?

I have turned my health around, but it was not easy, it was very hard to give up my two tomato sandwiches, Krystal cheeseburgers, and crackers in my soup. Giving up wheat, you will have withdrawal symptoms because it has a lot of chemicals in it. You are addicted to wheat and it is very hard to get off. After three or four months off wheat, I cheated and I stopped at the Krystal and ordered four Krystal cheeseburgers. I tore into two of them and I started feeling guilty. I threw the other two away.

After I regained my health, I was like a new preacher, I wanted to save everyone. Now I know I cannot do that. If I'm talking to someone and they say how bad they feel, I'll say, "Yes, I once was like that, but now since I got off wheat products, I feel great." If they start asking questions, I tell them more. If they do not respond, I drop the conversation. Friends who went wheat fee have told me after five days they could not stand it any longer and they went back to wheat. You could probably give up smoking easier than giving up wheat. After seven days it will get better giving up wheat. Remember, you must lead yourself to good health. A quote by Doctor Perlmutter, MD, in his book *Grain Drain*, says "most of us believe that we can live our own lives however we choose, and then when medical problems arise, we can turn to our doctors for a quick fix in the form of the latest and greatest pill." Dr. Perlmutter said, "Alzheimer's which presently has no cure, is preventable."

On January 25, 2014, I was reading the editorial section of our local newspaper, the *Rome News Tribune*. The main headline by Dick Yarbrough, our town columnist, was, "Who Wants to Live Longer Without Banana Pudding?" He says, "First off you should know American women have gone from being the longest-lived in the world in 1960s to 28th today." Whoa I wonder if it's the food. The information in the news report is attributed to a 2006 report from the National Academy of Sciences and a 2011 report from the National Institute of Health.

Up until the mid-fifties, people's greatest fears were polio, measles, chickenpox, and TB. If you hurt your leg and you told your parents, the first thing they thought was, "Has he got polio"? I remember Jerry Lewis hosting the March of Dimes and they would pick a young child that had polio and put there picture on these cards. It was usually a girl and she would be the poster child for the year. They would put these cards in stores and they had slots where you could put a dime into. They would also give us cards at school and we would take them home I would get mine filled up because if you did not you would fill guilty. When they were filled up you turn them in. This was a way to raise money to help fight polio. During World War II, our president, Franklin Roosevelt, had polio and spent a lot of time at Warm Springs, Georgia, better known as the Little White House. He went down to get relief for his legs and would sit in the hot springs and soak his legs in the water. During the war, FDR died in Warm Springs.

My dad had TB and they put him in Batty State Hospital in West Rome for several months. The federal government built it for wounded soldiers to be treated and after the war was over they gave it to the state. This was a very big hospital and there were lots of patients in the TB hospital. TB could be cured. Once you had polio, you had it the rest of your life. Years later after I was grown I came in contact with someone who had TB but they did not know it at the time. After a few weeks this person was at a get-together when I met him. A few weeks later he went to his doctor and found out he had TB. They called every one who had met him and we all had to take a pill every day for several weeks. That was the end of that. Later it became a mental hospital and today it is closed.

Why is cancer today our greatest fear? Today you go to the doctor and have tests ran and the doctor will tell you they will get back in touch with you in about a week. The first few days are not too bad but as each day goes by it gets worse. You wonder if it will be bad news that you have cancer or if everything is okay. After a week goes by, you cannot stand it any longer and you call your doctor. The doctor tells you, "Mr. Jones, your test results have not come back but we should be getting them back any day now." Now you really begin to get scared and worried now you think, if it takes this long it must really be bad. You do not sleep very well that night. The next day your doctor calls and you think what is he going to tell me. "Mr. Jones, we have your test results back and I need to discuss them with you. You need to be in my office at 4:00 p.m. tomorrow." You think, *Why not 8:00 a.m. or 9:00 a.m.?* The next day is the longest day of your life. You get there at 3:30 and wait and wait and finally, "Mr. Jones, the doctor will see you now." You are thinking, *Tell me yes or no*. He tells you that you have some minor problems and need to put you on some medication and in a few weeks you should be fine. Look what you went through to find out the good news.

Red Burkhalter, a good friend of mine, had his eye turn red and people told him, "I know of someone that had a problem like that and it was cancer and they died." Scared Red and made an appointment to see his doctor. Red went to see his doctor and the nurse said, "We need to take an x-ray of your eye," and they did. The nurse carried Red to his waiting room and a few minutes later she came back and said, "I have your x-rays" and stuck them inside of a folder on the door and she said, "The doctor will be in shortly to see you." The nurse left and Red got up, went over, got the x-ray out, and looked at it and he saw a big black spot in the area of his eye. Red thought, *Oh no, I do have cancer.* That scared him. He went back, sat down thinking the worst, and soon the doctor and nurse came in. The doctor picked up the x-ray and Red was watching for the reaction on his face. The doctor told the nurse this x-ray was no good and to get another x-ray. They did and Red had a small blood vessel that had burst in his eye and everything turned out good.

In 2006, my son, Sam Brannon, and his father in-law, Frank Groves, went to lunch at a local restaurant and while they were eating all of a sudden Frank started gagging, coughing, and foaming at the mouth. They both jumped up and ran to the bathroom and Frank kept doing it for about fifteen to twenty minutes. He finally stopped and they went and paid for their food and left. On the way home Sam said, "Frank, how long have you been doing that?"

He said, "For a pretty good while."

Sam said, "I want you to go see a doctor. That is not normal."
Frank said, "Okay, I will see one in a few days."

Frank made an appointment and in a few days went and saw his doctor. They ran a lot of tests on his esophagus and when it came back, he had cancer. About six weeks later Sam started having the same problems and he did not hesitate and made an appointment to see his doctor. Sam told the doctor what had happened to Frank and he had cancer and he wanted to get checked out as soon as possible. The doctor made Sam an appointment to come in and they would put him asleep to check his esophagus. They ran tubes down his throat and they cut out several polyps and when Sam woke up they told him what they had done. The doctor told Sam they would send them off and it would be two weeks before they would know the results. Sam knew Frank had cancer from the same thing and he was a nervous wreck for two weeks. As the two weeks drew to an end, it got even worse and finally the call came and the doctor said everything was okay. Not long after Frank died from cancer. You never hear anything about Polio today and cancer has taken the place of polio and is it for all the chemicals and whatever they are putting in our food? Chic-Fil-A announced within five years their chickens will be hormone free. Is this the beginning of good foods?

On March 23, 2014, in the *Rome New Tribune* Wizard of ID quote "wiz, my right eye twitches from time to time…you may have occasional twitchy right eye syndrome…here, take this once a day for the rest of your life…it's expensive, but we'll put you on a payment plan…oh, one of the side effects may cause your left eye to twitch…but I have something for you if that happens…follow up in six years…what was that… I've discovered modern medicine!"

What is in the food you are eating?

Remember, I have been there.

Why We Had to
Come Back to Rome

I'm a strong believer that everything has a purpose. We had a very young granddaughter, Gracie Byars, when Bobbie and I moved back to Rome in late 2008. Bobbie was needed because It was a very turbulent time in the family. Rob Byars, our son-in-law, was on drugs bad. Finally Rob hit rock bottom and one day he was sitting on his front porch when he prayed to God for help. And God responded. At that time Rob had nothing and I mean nothing and today I'm very proud of him. Soon afterward, Jacob Trent Byars was born a beautiful boy. When Gracie was born she had no hair or very little hair and JT came into the world with a head full of curly hair. Soon after Rob got his life together. Rob and I went up to Model High School to see Pepperell High School, a school me and Rob had both attended, to see our team play football. When we got to the ballpark I asked David Mathis if he would take me over to the Pepperell side because I was not able to walk over there. He had a golf cart and carried me. After the ball game, Rob and I left and while we were riding home, Rob said to me, "Were you not ashamed to be seen with me at the ballgame?"

I said, "Rob, I will be proud to be seen anywhere with you. I don't live in the past. There is nothing you can do about the past. You now live for the future and forget the past."

Crystal started to college to learn to be a Respiratory Therapist and she had to do a lot of studying and had to take a lot of tests. Bobbie and I raised Gracie and JT for two years because Crystal could not study with those two children around. Crystal passed and graduated as a respiratory therapist. Crystal now works at three different hospitals and she makes very good money. Rob started his own drywall business, which is called Rome Drywall, and he stays very busy. Rob also is a high school football official and he was invited to the Georgia Dome as a standby official in case someone got hurt. The Georgia Dome is where the final games of all high school teams that made it to the championship are played. Today Rob and Crystal live in a very nice home and drive nice cars. Bobbie and I are very proud of them.

My three sons Sam, Steve, and Joel have also done very good and Bobbie and I are very proud of them.

I might not like the way we had to come back to Rome to live. What I mean by that I broke my leg severely and had to file chapter 7 bankruptcy but it was meant to be.

If, If, If, If

I took a bitch to Harrah's Casino in Cherokee, North Carolina, and came back with an angel.

Bobbie called me on February 22, 2014 and said, "I am tired and ready for a break." She had been very tired and ill tempered. Her mom in Athens, Alabama, was sick and she had been up there several times taking care of her. About three weeks before this we were keeping the grandkids and Rob came by to pick up Gracie and Jacob. Bobbie started hollering, "They have destroyed my house and I am tired of them destroying my house." They had just scattered their toys all over the house and Papa Roy let them have their way. I thought she needed a break and we needed to get away so I called Bobbie back and I said, "Why don't we go up to Cherokee?" She said, "Okay. If we can't get a room at Harrah's Hotel I am not going." I said, "Okay, let me see what I can do."

It is only about a three-hour drive. I called Harrah's and they said they were fully booked and did not have any rooms at their feeder motels. I got on the computer and pulled up motels in Cherokee. I called the first one on the list, a Days Inn, and I know it is very close to the casino and I get Bill, who I could hardly understand. I asked, "Do you have any rooms available for tonight?" He said, "Where you need room?" (I think that's what he said) I said, "Cherokee," and he said, "Where's that?" I am looking at the computer and it shows the address and picture of the Days Inn and a phone number that I had just called, I hung up. I called the second one and I get another Bill who I definitely could not understand so I hung up. I called the third one and again I get another Bill who I could not understand. I finally found a motel with a local number. I called them and I made reservation for Saturday night. I am excited about finding us a place to stay. I call Bobbie and tell her, "I have found us a place to stay."

She said, "If it is not at Harrah's Hotel I am not going."

I said, "Bobbie, they are fully booked and all we need is just a place to sleep for a few hours."

She asked, "What is the name of the place?"

I said, "The Rivers Edge."

She said, "Okay. If it is not nice I am not going." She called back. "It looks okay, but if they do not have a shuttle to the casino I am not going."

I said, "I am sure they do." I really was not sure. I said, "Bobbie, let's try to leave around 3:00 p.m."

She said, "Do not tell me what to do and if you are going to rush me I am not going."

I kept my mouth shut and went home to get ready and waited on Bobbie to get ready. I never said a word about needing to hurry if we wanted to get there because it would give us very little time to play the slots. I was already ready and I just sat down and watched TV and I knew if I said anything she would say, "Don't rush me, if you do, I am not going."

We started our trip to Cherokee and the trip was okay. We get to the motel and check in to our room. The room was nice and very clean and I walked out on the balcony and straight down was the river. The river was clear and the water was moving very fast. We get settled in and Bobbie said, "I am not taking a bath in this bathroom."

I said, "Bobbie, what is wrong? It is very clean."

She said, "I just don't like it and I will not sleep here by myself. Check and see if they have a shuttle. If not, I am not going."

I went to the front desk and they gave me a phone number that I could call and it would cost five dollars for Wes to take us over.

She said, "Call him after I get ready." We then decided to drive over ourselves. We decided if we had too much to drink we would call a taxi. That was not a problem. Small, and I mean small, drinks were five dollars. We were in good shape to drive back. We lost our butts and went back to the motel. Next morning Bobbie took her bath. Afterward we drove back over to

Harrah's looking for a restaurant to eat breakfast and we pulled into what we thought was a restaurant. It was closed for the winter months and they were having a flea market in it. A lady said, "If you want a good breakfast, go to were you was at and a couple blocks down, there's a pancake breakfast restaurant."

We drove back over to where we had stayed and a couple blocks from the motel was the restaurant. We walked in about 9:30 and there a very good crowd of people inside. We knew this would be a good place to eat. The waiters were very friendly and they gave us a menu. I looked it over and there was only one thing that did not have pancakes on the menu. I had steak and eggs and no bread. While I was waiting on my food, I got to looking around and at least 80 percent of the people were overweight. That's what eating all that bread and syrup will do for you. Bobbie was now my angel and on our way home, Bobbie said, "Look at those chicken houses, they do not have any windows in them." There were three large fans on the side of the building to blow fresh air in. Now I know what they mean with chickens being raised in buildings that are pitch black.

After we got home Sunday afternoon, Bobbie called Crystal and said, "Can the grandkids come over and spend the night?" Crystal said yes, and they came over and we all had a good time. Monday I had to go to Felton, Georgia, south of Cedartown, to meet James Paxton, a friend of ours.

Bobbie was raised in Felton and she went to school with James and was neighbors with the Paxtons. Bobbie helped take care of Velma Paxton, James's mother. We had left a heater down there and I was going to get it. James lived in Florida and he was only going to be there for a short period of time. James said, "Can you meet me before lunch?" I said yes. I was working on my book and I looked at the time and it was 11:08. I thought I have got to go now and I decided to make copies. I thought I had to go. I left East Rome and started down US 27 toward Felton and about seven miles south of Rome I came upon a very bad wreck. There were about ten cars ahead of me. It was at least five or more minutes before other emergency vehicles got to the wreck. A sheriff's car was just ahead of me and he happened to come up on the wreck. An ambulance was sitting in the northbound lane. Evidently he just happened to come up on the wreck. It was a Chevy King cab truck headed north to go to Floyd hospital to see his son who was going to have surgery. According to Rome News, he wrecked and rolled over several times into the southbound lanes for a quarter mile. The driver was thrown out and died. The wreck happened at 11:15 and I left my house around 11:08. I believe my guardian angel was with me one more time.

In early 2014, I was having very sharp pain in my bad leg where I had broken it. I called Denise at Workers Comp. and told her about the pain I was having. Denise said it was probably due to the cold wet winter we were having. I said yes, and I will give it a few months to see if the pain would go away. About six weeks later, I walked out to get my mail and after I got the mail I turned and walked a short distance and my leg locked up on me. If I moved I would had very sharp pain in my bad leg and I could not move. There was no one at home and I wondered what I was going to do. I needed crutches to get back in the house, but no one was around. I almost called 911 but about that time it broke loose and I was able to hobble back into the house. I called Denise and told her what happened and that I needed to see Dr. Lundy. Denise said, "Okay, go ahead and call him and make an appointment," which I did. A few weeks later I saw Dr. Lundy and he x-rayed my leg and he said, "I don't see anything wrong but let's do an MRI on that leg to make sure." A few weeks later I had the MRI done and I took the results back to Dr. Lundy. Dr. Lundy looked at it and said, "I don't see anything wrong but you must have a bone chip or scar tissue causing the problem." Dr. Lundy said, "I want you to go to physical therapy two times a day for six weeks and let them break it loose." Now to break something loose was going to be very painful. I was overcompensating from my bad leg to my good leg. I went to Floyd County Rehabilitation Center in Rome, Georgia, and Josh or Joy would work on my bad leg. Joy was gentle when she worked on my leg but Josh was a different story. Josh would take his thumb, press down on the side of my leg next to that seven-inch scar where they took that plate out of my leg. When he hit that scar tissue, the pain was very bad and I would almost jump off the table. They would put small patches on my leg and shoot electrons into my leg for fifteen minutes. After twelve trips the sharp pain went away and now my bad leg is my good leg and my good leg is now my bad leg. I am having lots of pain in the knee of my former good leg. When I would go down steps I would lead off with my bad leg and put the weight on my good leg but now it is reversed. I favor my former good leg.

I checked my sugar for several days for the first time in months. It averaged around 140. I started listening to Bobbie and she would say, "Just a little bit won't hurt you." Well, a little bit will hurt you. I strayed off my diet and it showed up. I am now back on my diet and my blood sugar is normal. It is almost impossible to stay on it. I only know four people who are doing what I do. I am determined to have good health. Only I can do it.

I enjoy my two small grandkids. Gracie, six, and Jacob Trent (JT) Byars, five, keep me busy. The Seventh Son is still going.

I was watching Fox House Call on Fox News on July 6, 2014, and the doctors said in 2010 twenty-six million people were diabetic and today there are 29.1 million people who have diabetes. The doctors said two-thirds of the population is overweight or obese. Today lots of young people are becoming diabetic due to the foods they are eating and lack of exercise. Where are you in this group? There is hope. Start reading good books and eating good foods.

Today, out of eight boys and three girls, Glenn and I are the only two left standing, as well as Jean, Glenn's wife, Dayton Miller, Barbara's husband, and Brenda, Grady's wife.

Acknowledgment

Special thanks to my brother Glenn Brannon and my friend Sarah Burkhalter for helping with this book.

Epilogue

- Charles Cliff Brannon, born June 3, 1897, passed away in Rome, Georgia, on May 24, 1967
- Grace Brannon, born August 16, 1901, passed away in Rome, Georgia, on June 28, 1967
- Sarah Brannon, born January 19, 1911, passed away in Tucson, Arizona, on September 16, 1999
- John Brannon, born April 10, 1921, passed away in Jackson, South Carolina, on July 2, 2010
- George "Doc" Brannon, born January 9, 1923, passed away in Rome, Georgia, on March 4, 1995
- James "Shag" Brannon, born July 28, 1924, passed away in Rome, Georgia, on September 3, 2001
- Charles "Happy" Brannon, born October 19, 1927, passed away in Cedartown, Georgia, on August 3, 1957

- Jewell Brannon, born September 8, 1929, passed away in Norfolk, Virginia, on February 9, 1999
- Glenn Brannon, born October 31, 1934, lives in southern Floyd County
- Earl Brannon, born October 8, 1936, passed away in Rome, Georgia, on March 29, 2003
- Roy B. Brannon, born April 4, 1940, lives in Rome, Georgia
- Barbara Brannon, born February 16, 1941, passed away in Tucson, Arizona, on July 16, 1991
- Grady Brannon, born November 22, 1943, passed away in Rome, Georgia, on May 23, 2003

Front Row (left to right): Sara Brooks, Betty Calloway, Louise Carter, Fay Formby, Glenda Cobb, Mildred Emma Bell, Shirley Dempsey, Miss Fannie Sproull, Teacher. Second Row: Shirley Barton, Janette Bennett, Bonnie Bramlett, Bertha Ball, Glenda Fox, Lucile Foshee. Third Row: Albert Burkhalter, Robert Bates, Cox, Roy Brannon, David Dixon, Paul Brown, Jerry Brandon, Jackie Brooks, David Baker. Fourth Row: Lowell Curry, Charles Dean, David Bohannon, Richard Beam, Roger Carney, Wilburn Bevels, Anthony Byars, Roney Broom.

Front Row (left to right): Jo Nelle Batey, Linda Bailey, Dorothy Abernathy, Martha Brown, Yvonne Ashworth, May Ann Dorby, Lynda Broom. Second Row: Sara Ruth Bonner, Charlotte Garrett, Carolyn Jones, Jane Bradshaw, Charlotte Bennett, Barbara Brannon, Ann Bohannon, Barbara Alston. Third Row: Glenn Bowling, Cleveland Adams, Gene Ford, Glenn Childress, James Childress, Eddie Shaw. Fourth Row: James Melvin Blue, Charles Collins, Bobby Covington, Max Akins, Kenneth Brannon.

This is the house I was born in

Roy Bradie Brannon

Sarah John Doc Shag Glenn Earl Roy Grady

Roy Bradie Brannon

Grady

Roy Bradie Brannon